Breaking Free Too:

TAKING A FLIGHT WITH A BUTTERFLY TOWARD SELF-DISCOVERY

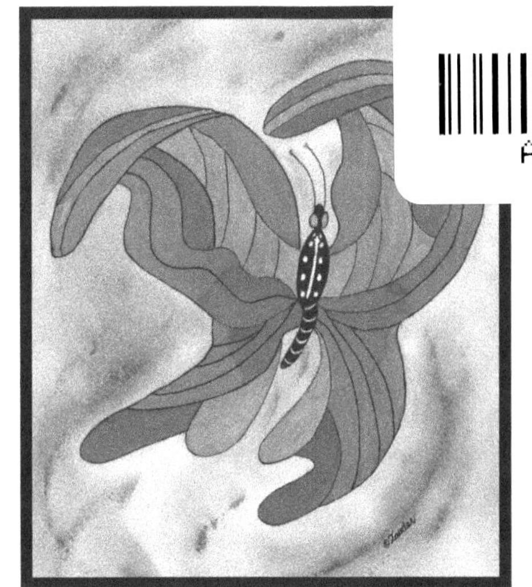

Written and illustrated by
Tamara Lauder M.D.

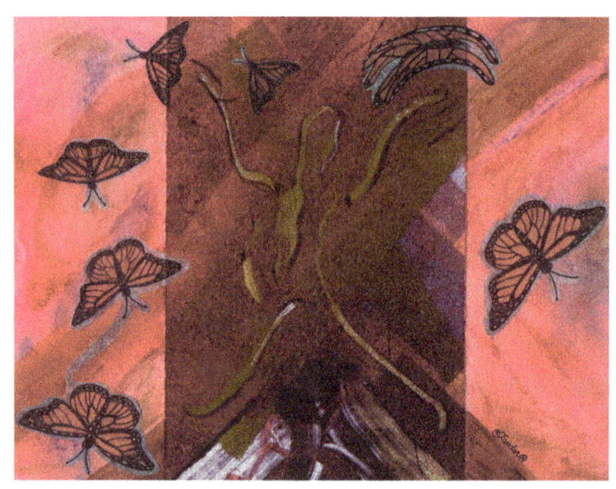

About the Title: *Breaking Free Too*

Breaking Free Too is the title of the book and of an illustration within the book. The illustration entitled *Breaking Free Too* is a mixed-medium artwork inspired by an earlier monotype created by the author and artist in 2002 entitled *Breaking Free*. Both symbolize breaking free from what binds us, similar to the butterfly.

Cover Art: *Flying Free*

Flying Free is a watercolor created by
Tamara Lauder of T.Lauder Pottery & Printmaking.
Flying Free symbolizes the freedom obtained
with self-discovery.

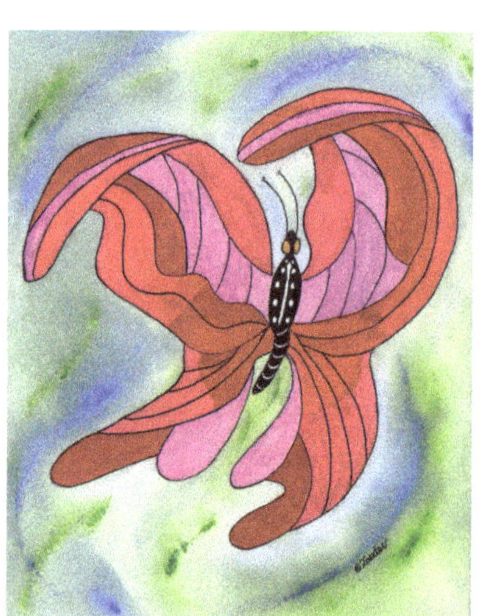

Breaking Free Too:

TAKING A FLIGHT WITH A BUTTERFLY TOWARD SELF-DISCOVERY

by Tamara Lauder, M.D.

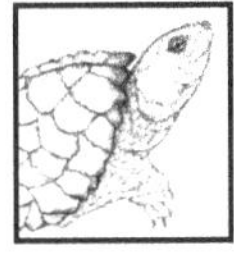

Turtleye Publishing
St. Germain, WI

turtleyepub@yahoo.com

ISBN# 978-0-9860829-0-0
Library of Congress Control Number: 2014919168

All Book and Cover Illustrations by Tamara Lauder
Cover and Book Design by Lori Hahn and Chad Skubal
Printed in the United States of America
Hahn Printing, Inc., Eagle River, Wisconsin

Table of Contents

Acknowledgements

First and foremost, I acknowledge all of the people who I have cared for and all of the people who have cared for me. It is your influences on my life that provide the content for this book. I especially acknowledge my husband and best friend in life, Jeff Lauder. Not only was he integral in assisting with the artistic and written creative process of this book, but his unconditional love and support makes every moment in life a pleasant adventure worth experiencing.

To my dear friends Carmen Farwell, and Barbara Johnson, I thank you for your listening ear and always helpful suggestions. I thank Carmen Farwell, Buddy Bess, Dee Thatcher, and Lori Hahn for their editorial and publishing guidance. To the unselfish authors who shared their writing and publishing experiences with me, I thank you—in particular, Donna Winters, Deborah Frontiera, John Bates, Leon "Buckshot" Anderson, and Robert Metropulos.

Introduction

One sunny summer day as I was approaching the house, I noticed two butterflies resting in front of my door. Clearly unthreatened by my presence, over five minutes passed before they gently flew away and allowed me to enter. While their literal presence was a mere five minutes, their impression was long lasting.

Why were those butterflies so interested in that particular spot on my front porch on that particular day? What made them so unafraid? The answers to those questions remain a mystery. Nature is beautiful and mysterious as a result of an orchestration of many individual parts playing their unique role. The orchestration of nature demonstrates the powerful and positive effect that carrying out one's individual true potential has on the world. If everything in nature looked the same, sounded the same, and had the same purpose, it would not have the significant emotional impact on us that it does. Nature is the consummate storyteller. If we listen carefully, it generously offers the story of mankind's journey on earth. Those butterflies had an emotional impact on me that day. I realized that they had a story to tell that I must share.

The book you are about to read, is my transcription of the butterfly's story to us. I call it *Breaking Free Too: Taking a Flight With a Butterfly Toward Self-Discovery* because the butterfly teaches us just that—how to break free from what binds us and fly free as the unique human beings that we are created to be. Using the butterfly as an allegory, this book uses three ways to communicate its message. On each page, symbolic artwork, interpretive titles, and accompanying short text address the journey of life, the influences that affect how we see ourselves and the decisions we make, the obstacles we face throughout life, and the help available to us. Each of these three communication methods allows for a unique and independent reading experience by providing a visually symbolic interpretation, a short story, and an in-depth and calculating reflection. It is a book of awareness, not answers, intended to stimulate you to ask and answer difficult questions for yourself, with a goal of helping you unlock your own mystery and find greater fulfillment in life.

The artwork created for this book is bright, colorful, and childlike. I made it childlike because it is in our youth that we really know who we are, but external pressures and life circumstances often force us to leave that person behind. While I offer examples of how the life of a butterfly parallels our own, each piece of artwork is symbolic and meant for you to apply to yourself, your circumstances, and your own life journey. Any page read individually provides a powerful concept and short story by itself. Read cover to cover, all of the concepts coalesce to provide a reflective and colorful pictorial story about becoming our true self.

Are you using your talents and doing what you were made to do? Or, do you feel trapped, blocked, afraid, and unable to become the person inside of you, nagging at your soul, and waiting to break free? Like the butterfly, what makes us who we are is multifaceted. As you look at and read this allegory, take the time to self-reflect so that you too, like the butterfly, can break free and fly.

General Themes

Several general themes are symbolized in the details of each piece of artwork in this book. In particular, the circular and convoluted shape of the tree with an opening toward the sky, the placement of the different stages of butterfly development within the tree, and the surrounding environment as well as the things within it, all provide purposeful imagery. Think of the themes listed below as you look at each picture and read.

The physical life cycle of a butterfly and the emotional journey of man follow a cyclic pattern.

We are forever intertwined with our roots.

It is a convoluted journey toward our first flight.

We start out life higher in the tree (egg).

As we grow and mature (larval/caterpillar stage), we descend back toward our roots—exploring, crawling, and scrounging for nourishment from the entire environment that we are exposed to.

Tired, we settle back to a comfort zone and become inactive for a while. We exist within the boundaries of what we know, all the while undergoing a silent metamorphosis (pupal stage).

Slowly, we break free from what binds us—those things that hold us captive and prevent our wings from expanding.

We hold on tightly to the familiar and comfortable, despite the fact that our wings for first flight have developed.

We must move within the convoluted journey that lies before us, all the while gaining strength to leave our familiar environment, to the strange and large new world that lies all around us.

As we spread our wings and fly, we expose ourselves to the mysterious and liberating world that offers us the opportunity to become the full person we are created to be.

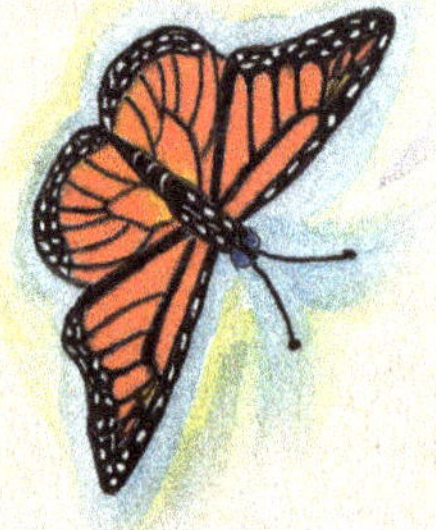

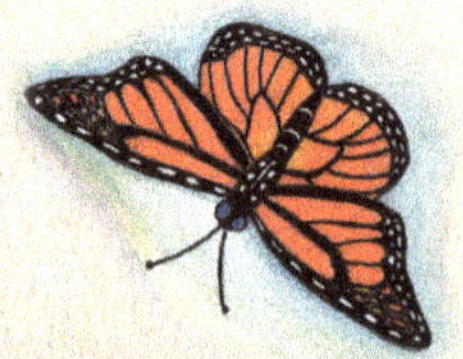

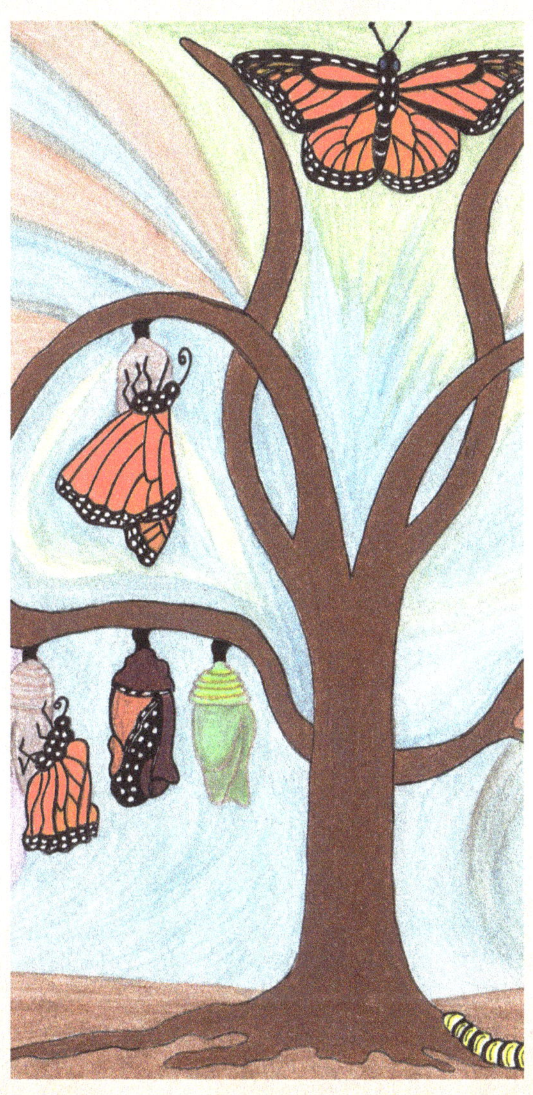

Section One
The Cycles of Life

The symbolism reflected by each developmental stage of the butterfly, which leads to its first flight, conveys a unique and individual message to each one of us. It is unique and individual because each of us exists emotionally and spiritually at a different place at any given point in life. We do not each follow the same path or the same timeline. Some people are clear about who they are and where their life's journey has taken, or will take them. Others wander for a while or for a lifetime in search of their true selves.

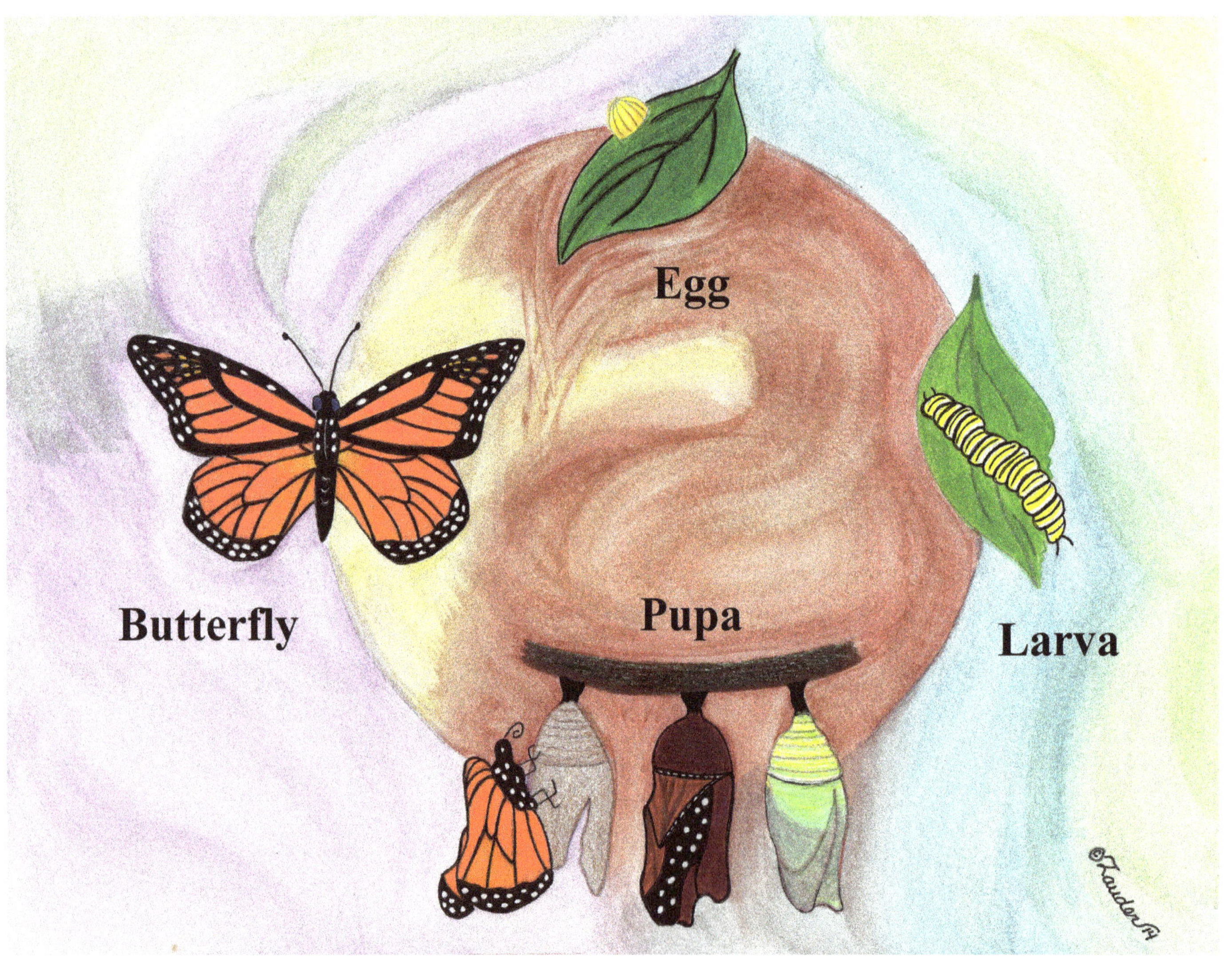

Egg
Larva
Pupa
Butterfly

THE BUTTERFLY LIFE CYCLE
"Life is a cycle."

Let's begin the reflection of our lives with a brief overview of the stages of a butterfly's physical development.[1] The life cycle of a butterfly consists of four stages which repeat themselves in a cyclic pattern in nature. At each stage, one form of the butterfly ceases to exist as it transforms into the next living form required for the development of a four-winged butterfly.

A butterfly begins, in its most primitive form, as an egg. While pictured as a single egg, a female butterfly may lay more than one egg at a time, usually placing them somewhere in nature such as the leaf of a plant.

The life form inside the egg emerges as a caterpillar. The caterpillar stage is also known as the larval stage.

Once the caterpillar has completed its necessary course on earth and completed its maturity, it settles down and enters the pupal, or chrysalis, stage of its life. It is during this stage of the life cycle that the most significant physical transformation takes place in the butterfly's development. This transformation is known as metamorphosis.

Finally, what started out as a tiny unnoticed egg emerges from the chrysalis as a beautiful four-winged butterfly. Although illustrated here most closely resembling a monarch, these stages occur in a similar fashion for all butterfly species.

The details of each stage of a butterfly's physical development closely resemble what takes place in the emotional and spiritual development and transformation within the human species. Similar to the life cycle of the butterfly, our emotional and spiritual journey occurs in a cyclic pattern throughout our lifetime. It is a personal journey in which one leaves the old for the new. It is a cycle which requires us to leave behind old learned restraints that bind us, in order to move forward in life and open our wings and fly into the big new world.

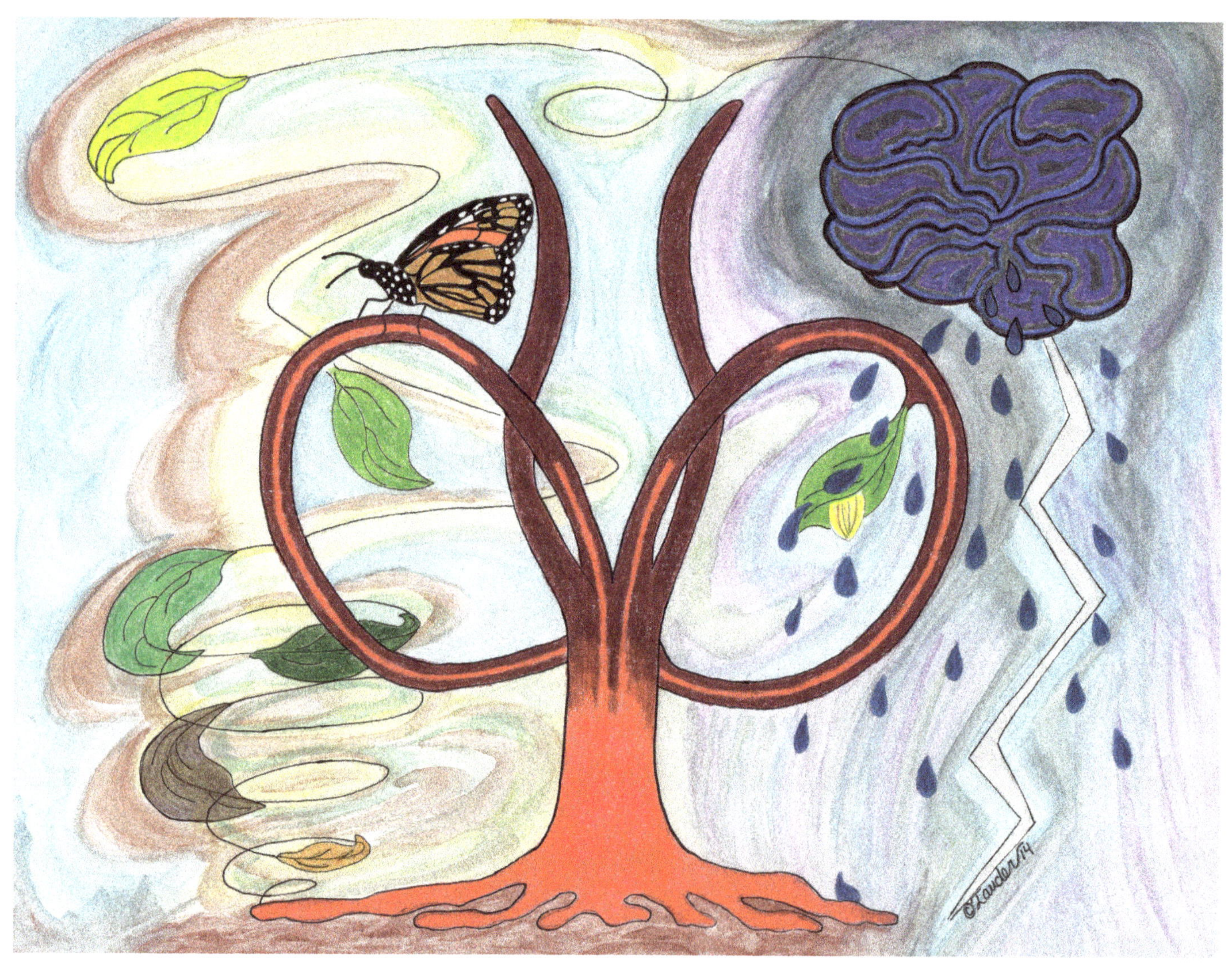

THE EGG: EXPECTED AND PROTECTED
"We begin life with great expectations."

Both the butterfly and humans start out life as an egg. The butterfly egg has a hard outer shell and is usually carefully placed in an inconspicuous spot in nature, often the underside of a leaf—defenses which are important to protect it from the many environmental stresses and predators to which it is exposed. There are great expectations for the tiny egg. The egg is expected to become a butterfly with the same colors, habits, and behaviors of the adult butterfly of its species, only adapting to environmental changes over time for survival.

Like the butterfly egg's hard outer shell, we too start out life with an outer shell that protects us from outside pressures and dangers, ensuring that we progress to the next developmental stage. Our outer shell is represented by a variety of protectors. Initially, it is the womb, the place beyond our control and vulnerable to influences that cannot be modified by us. After birth, it might be the people who cradle and love us as their own. Other times, our shell is a shield that we develop for ourselves over time—a shield that guards us from the negative aspects of life and becomes a necessary component for our survival instinct.

Similar to the butterfly, our lives too begin with great expectations, sometimes placed upon us before we are even a fertilized egg. When we are still a preconceived notion in the minds of our parents, plans, hopes, and anticipations have already been placed upon us. Once we become a reality as a developing child in our mother's womb, the expectations placed upon us begin and continue on after birth. Before we are old enough to process information or put anything into context with who we really are, people and things outside of us place great expectations on who and what we are to become. Expectations stem from our family unit, our ancestors, culture, and the environment and social structure in which we live.

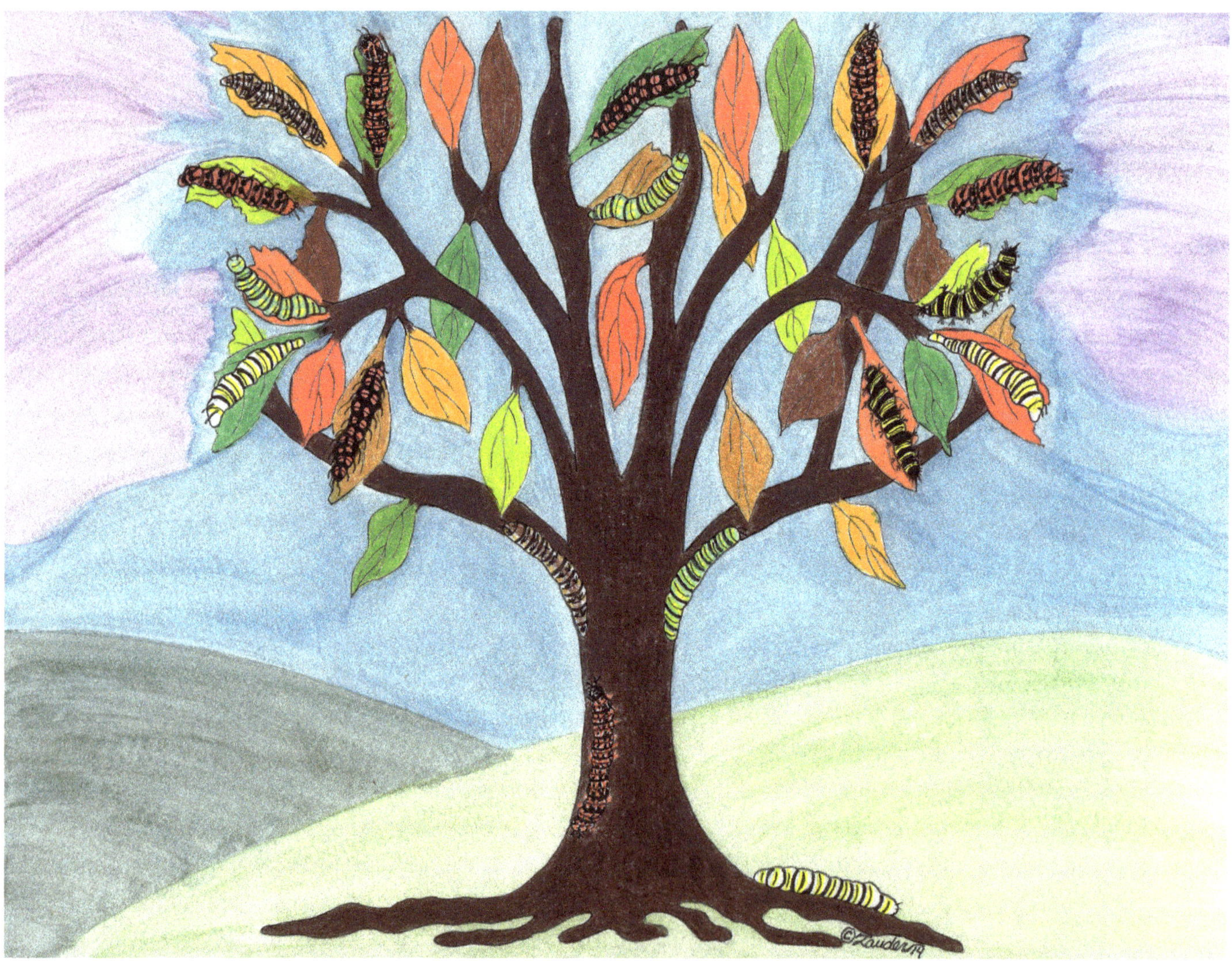

Larval Stage/Caterpillar: Crawling & Eating
"We take it all in and digest what we can."

The butterfly egg hatches as a larva, better known as a caterpillar. During this stage, the caterpillar attends to the basic physiologic needs required for its next stage of development. It spends a lot of time eating and storing energy. As it eats, it grows. In order for the caterpillar to continue to fit inside its skin as it grows, it must molt, or shed, its old skin several times. With each molt, the caterpillar begins to take on its own unique appearance and color which distinguish it from other caterpillars. The colors and unique features that an individual caterpillar develops with each molt are not only due to predetermined genetic factors, but also develop in response to the environment to which it is exposed and must survive within.

Like the molting caterpillar, we begin to show a bit of our own unique colors and features at a very early stage of life. We are each born with certain inherent personality features and our own individual emotional profile, but what is inherent for us, may or may not be nurtured by those around us or by our environmental circumstances and opportunities. In fact, our natural inclinations and emotional needs may be so different from the people around us that they may be unaware of our specific needs, and therefore, unable to provide the developmental support we require.

As humans, we move through a "larval" stage by consuming information from our surroundings, processing both positive and negative feedback. As our brains process the information, reactions, and feedback that we have been exposed to, we grow. With each growth period, we shed some of what we knew or learned previously, not only in reaction to the responses that we have encountered, but also according to how our individual personalities perceive things. With each growth and "molt" of our previous skin, we "change color" a little and develop additional features that help protect our hearts and emotions, and keep us safe from emotional and physical danger.

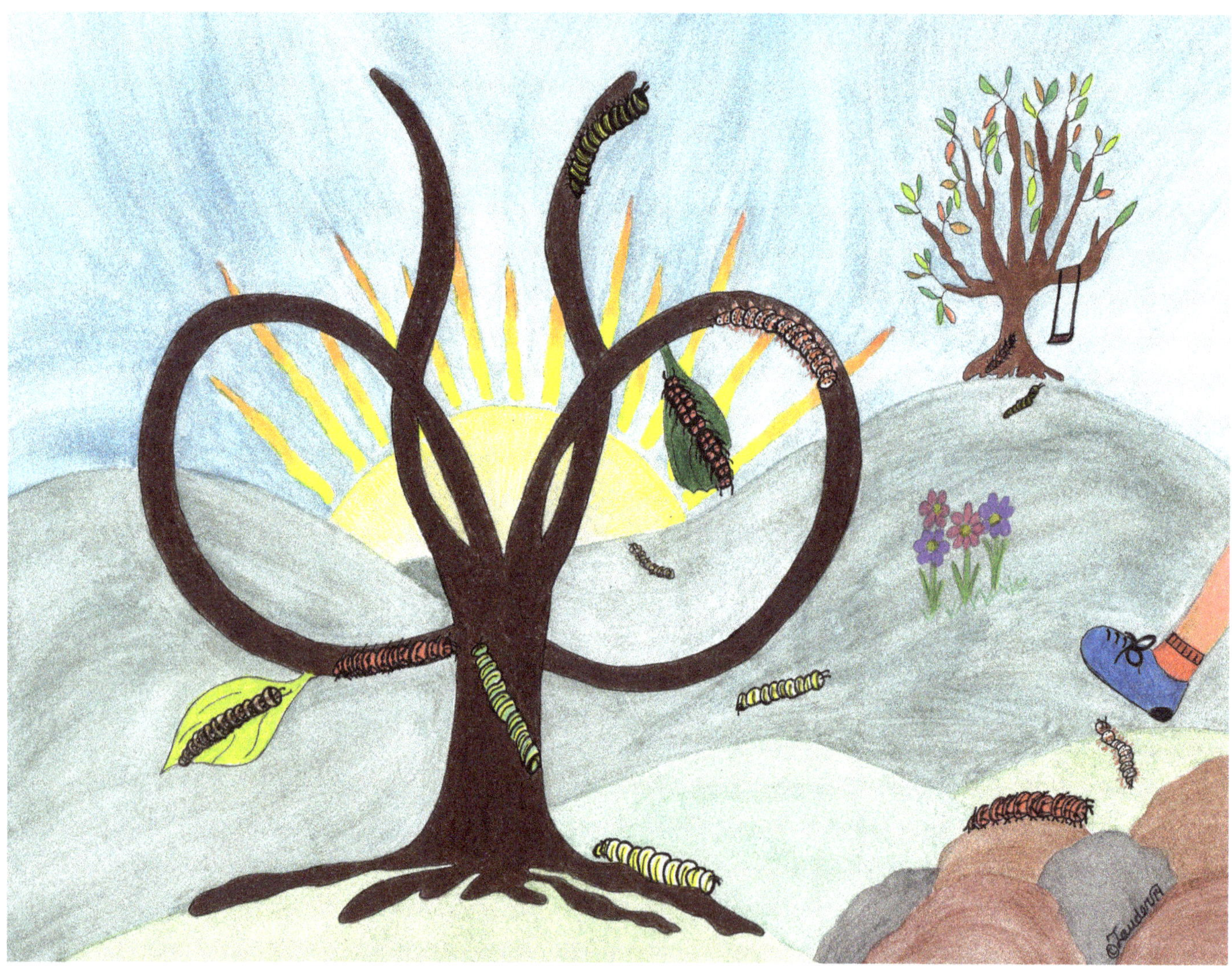

Larval Stage/Caterpillar: The Great Explorer
"We learn as we go."

During the larval stage of development, not only does the caterpillar eat a lot, but it spends a great amount of time exploring all aspects of its environment. Both caterpillars and humans have something called an intrinsic system made up of hormones and a central nervous system, which includes the brain. This intrinsic system responds to both the body's internal environment, as well as the external environment, making up the survival instinct necessary for self-preservation. The timing of the larvae to begin the next stage of development depends on its response to its personal internal and external environments.

Similar to the caterpillar, we spend time in our life observing, experiencing, and absorbing the environment around and within us. All of our previous experiences, environments, and our intrinsic system affect how and when we move forward in our development. Our experiences act as a catalyst—the information—that initiates a series of self-regulating feedback systems. That means that our life experiences evoke both physiological and mental responses to help defend us from changes which might disrupt our body's internal and external environments. All of these internal and external factors interplay and influence how each of us emotionally and spiritually develops, and how our genetic code expresses itself. The world that we explore and experience affects our physical, emotional, and spiritual well-being both positively and negatively.

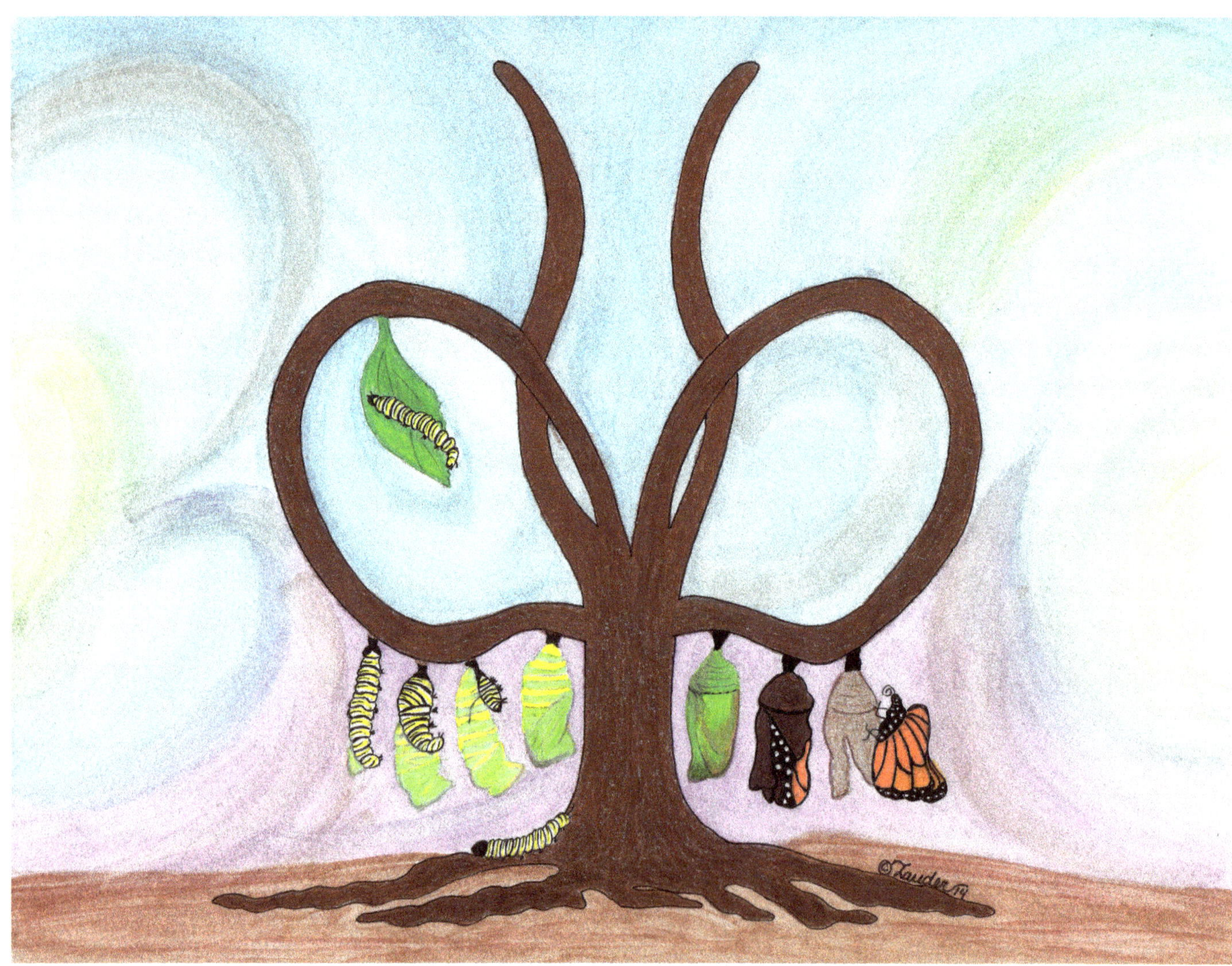

Pupal Stage/Chrysalis[2]: Silent Metamorphosis
"We transform even though we cling to what we know."

In the third stage of a butterfly's physical development, the caterpillar sheds its skin one last time to reveal the pupa. At this stage, the caterpillar stops eating and exploring. The pupal stage is an inactive stage of the life cycle of the butterfly, even though complex metamorphic changes are occurring inside the encapsulated object called a chrysalis. Inside the chrysalis, the caterpillar parts are broken down and dissolved until it no longer looks like a caterpillar. Butterfly structures develop. Once the butterfly is fully developed, it will not emerge from the chrysalis until again, both its internal and external environments are suitable. Then, the chrysalis splits open, and the fully developed butterfly emerges.

Similar to the once curious and hungry caterpillar that stops eating and exploring, at different points in our life, we too may become inactive and remain bound by the protective coating of the familiar. We might stop exploring and taking in new information because of previous reactions from our environment and the people in it. We abandon our dreams and hopes about developing into the people we imagined we could or wanted to be. Like a caterpillar inside a chrysalis, we too move inside ourselves, clinging to what we know and have learned. Often we become what others want or need us to be. Our parts are broken down like the caterpillar parts in the pupa, and we become unrecognizable from the enthusiastic individual that we once were. Despite our perceived inactivity, however, we are using our previous experiences and undergoing a dramatic metamorphosis, requiring a huge amount of energy.

The newly emerged butterfly clings to the empty shell of a chrysalis because it is not yet strong enough to fly on its own. At this point, the tightly bound morphology of the butterfly does not allow the world to see it for the beautiful, distinct adult butterfly that it is meant to be. Likewise, we emerge from the inactive, and perhaps uneasy, time of our life with all of our distinct, beautiful, and unique colors and features. Tired and weak from all of the energy required for our silent transformation, we remain in a tightly bound morphology clinging to our zone of comfort. We are not yet strong enough to let go.

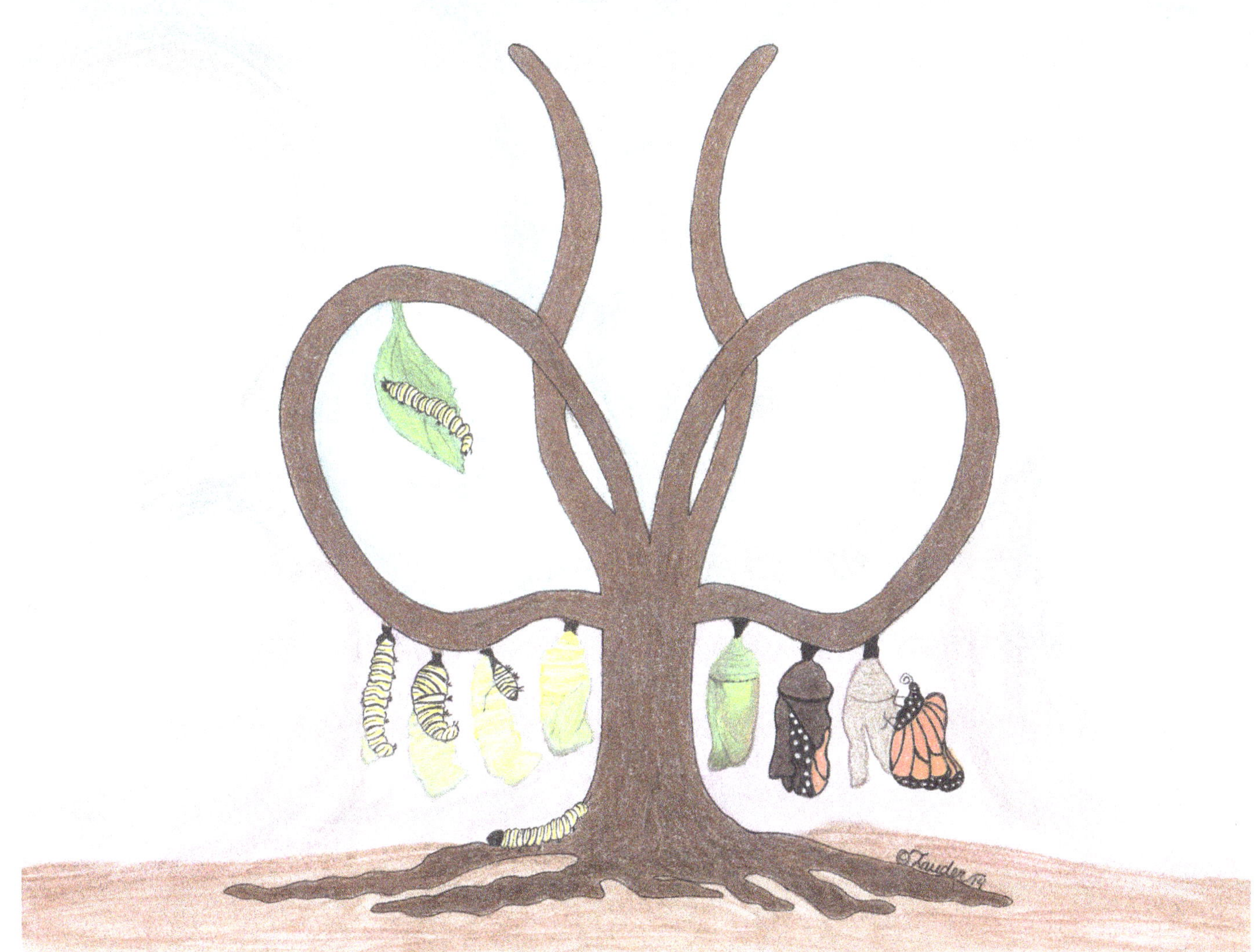

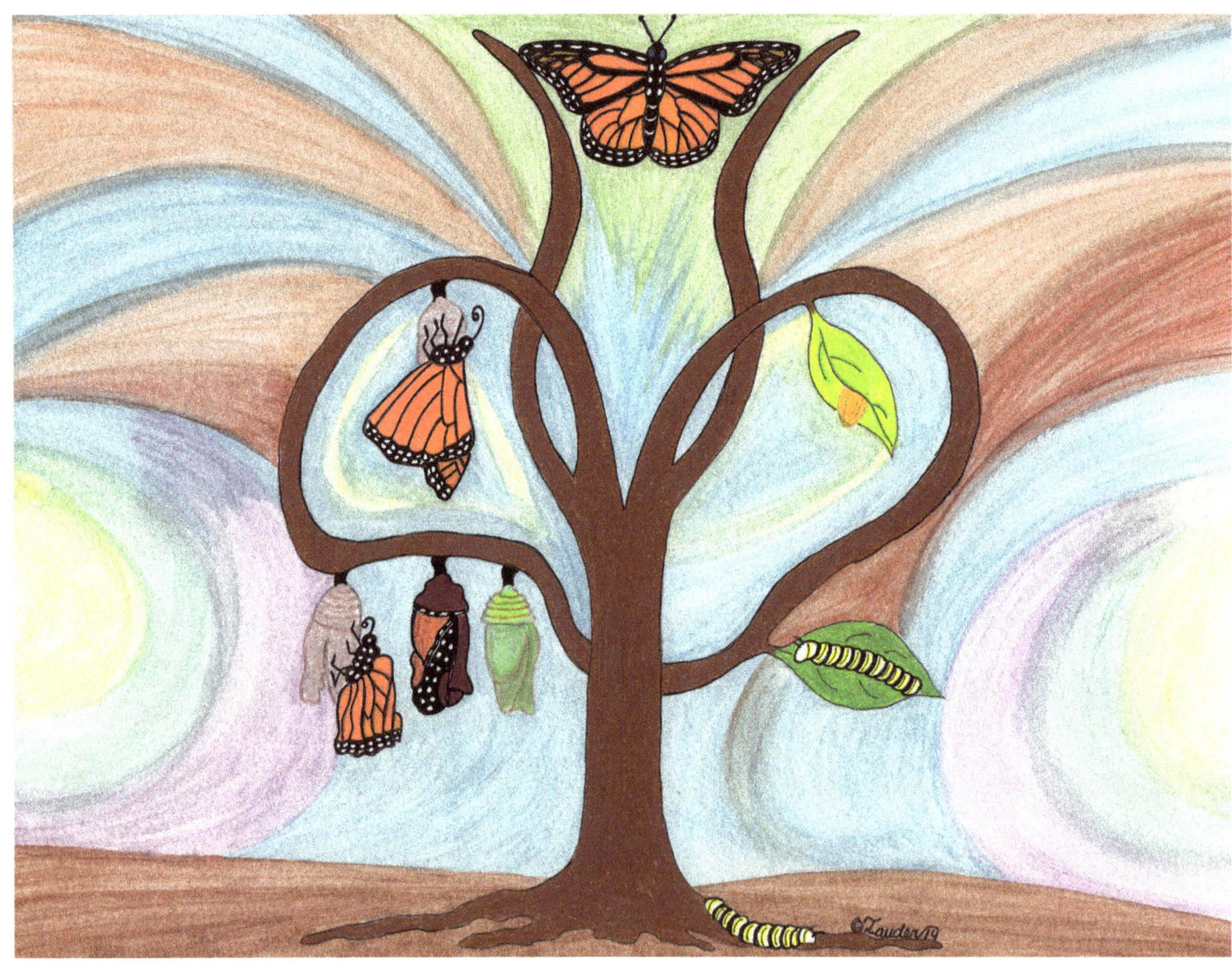

BUTTERFLY: FIRST RELEASE
"Our opening ceremony. It feels right to launch."

The term metamorphosis refers to a change in the structure and habits of an animal during normal growth. For the butterfly, metamorphosis includes transformation from an egg to a caterpillar to a chrysalis to a four-winged butterfly. Metamorphosis requires a lot of food, patience, and the appropriate environment and timing. After this transformation, the tightly-bound butterfly rests for a while and gains enough strength to open its colorful wings, let go of the open chrysalis, and fly for the first time.

As with the butterfly, we carry the complete package of our genetic material through all stages of life. What alters the rate and behavior of our metamorphosis is similar to the butterfly—our respective internal and external environments and our perceptions and reactions to those environments. We emerge from the inactive but inner growth periods of our life with all of the necessary elements to break free from what binds us. At this point, the world, and often ourselves, are unable to see us for who we really are, what we are capable of, and what we were designed to become. In order for the world to see our true beauty and colors, we must release ourselves from our tightly bound morphology. We must rest, rejuvenate, and take the time for self-reflection. Self-reflection requires quiet and discipline and is a necessary component of self-discovery. Once we gain enough strength, we can open our wings, let go of our chrysalis—our zone of comfort but the place that holds us tight—and fly for the first time.

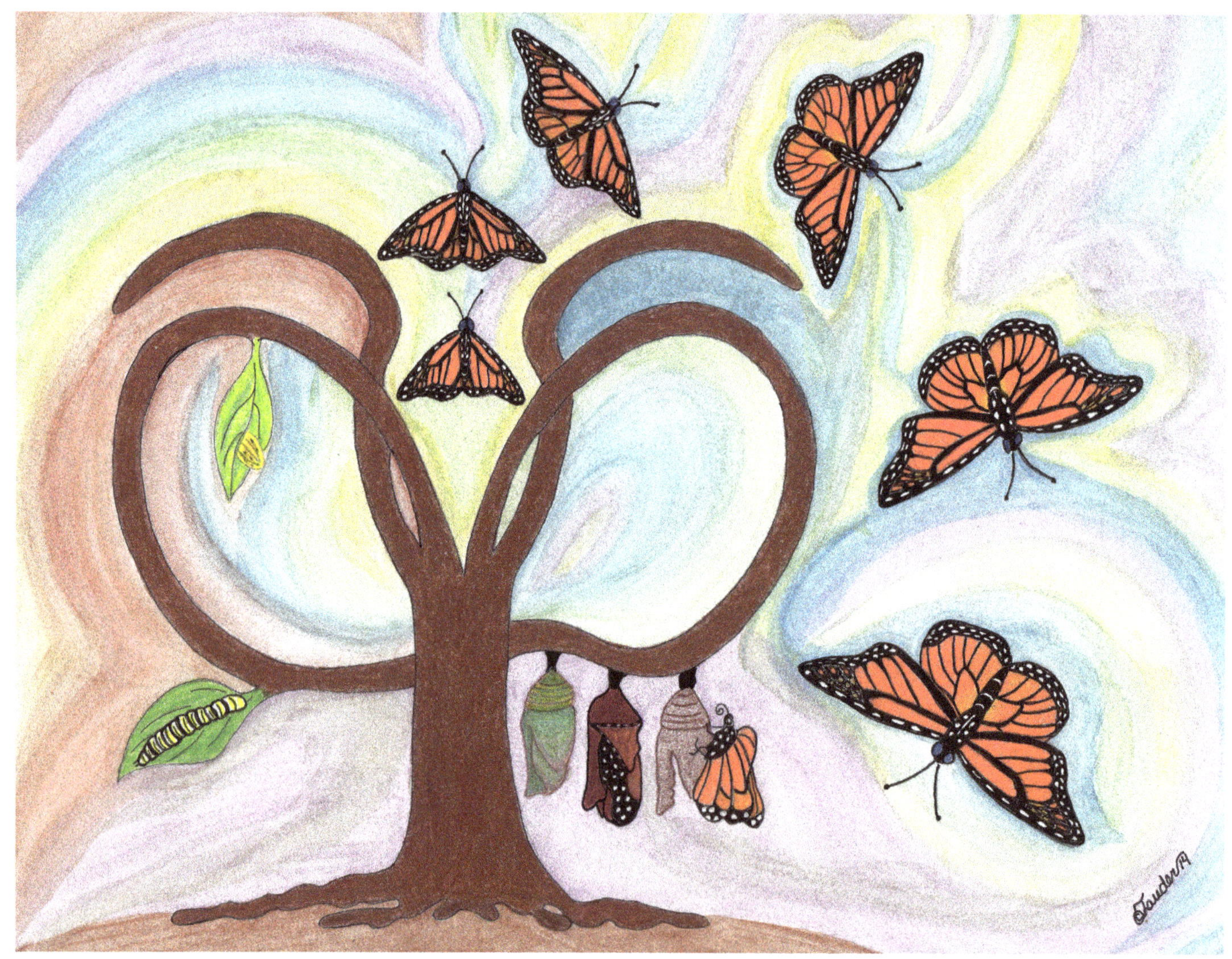

BUTTERFLY: THE EXODUS
"Leaving our place of comfort can be scary but liberating."

At last! The butterfly lets go of the chrysalis, opens its wings, and flies away from its place of safety. It spreads its beautiful wings and flies freely and independently into the vast new world. It uses its instincts and sensory organs to assess the world around it and search out a desirable and suitable habitat.

Similar to each individual butterfly, the time that it takes to build our strength and let go of our securities varies with each of us. For some people, it takes only a short time to recognize that personal restraints exist, and they are able to move beyond those restraints fairly quickly. Others may never recognize that either themselves or their surroundings prevent them from growing and moving beyond the things in life that act as the chrysalis to which they continue to tightly cling. Yet for others, despite recognizing the things that keep them bound or stagnant in the same comfortable or uncomfortable place in life, it takes months, years, or even a lifetime to let go and move forward. Often, the biggest and only obstacles in our way are our own fears or irrational perceptions. Other times, it is the choices we have made, our personal circumstances, situations that we cannot responsibly walk away from, cultural, or socioeconomic circumstances and expectations.

Each person walks a different journey in life that is uniquely their own. Some, who are vulnerable enough to share their experiences, may find others who can relate, understand, and empathize. For others, their personal journey is so unique that few will share a similar experience. Regardless of where we find ourselves on our own journey, we all have the opportunity to rest, gain the necessary strength, let go, and fly freely and independently.

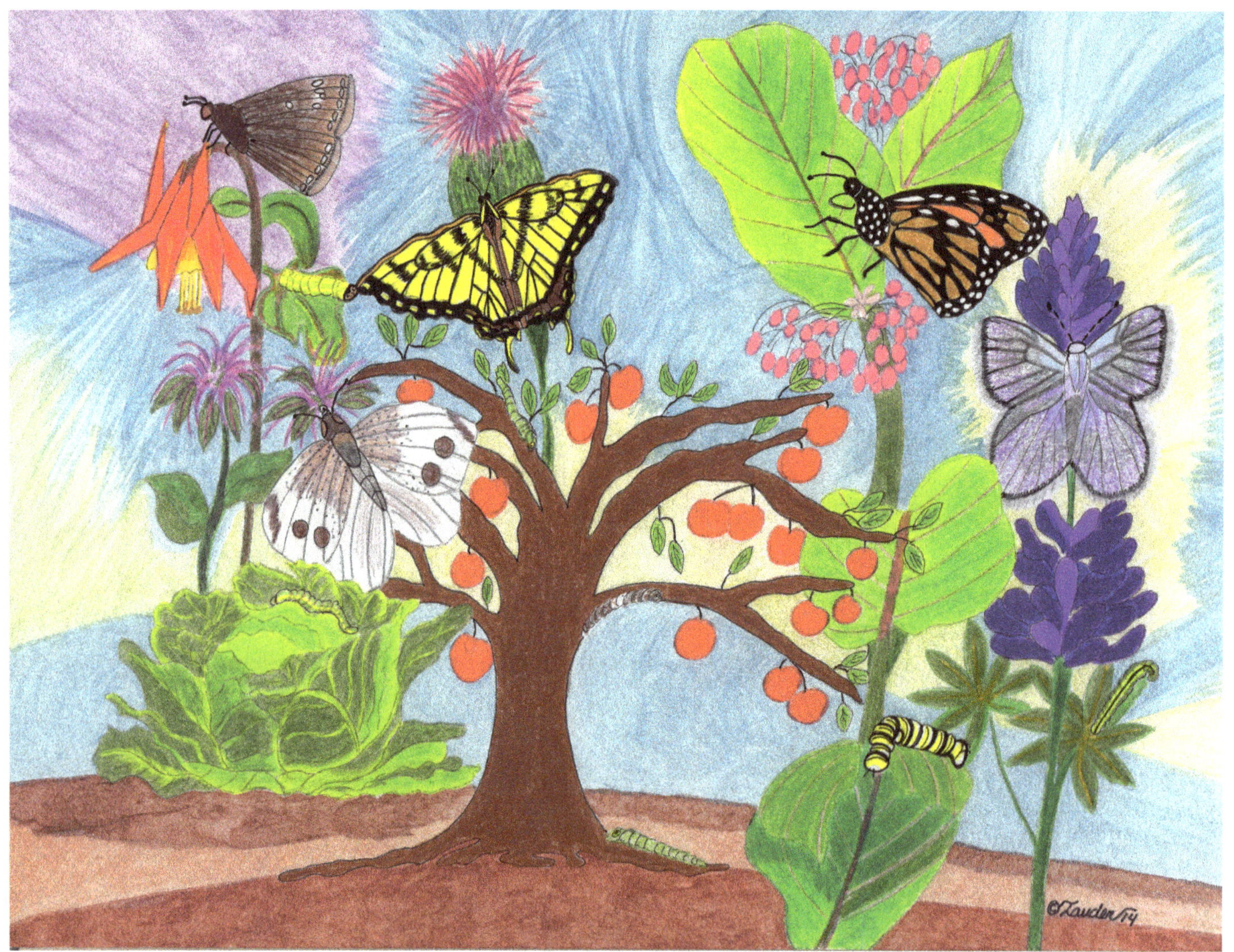

BUTTERFLY: FOOD FOR SUCCESS
"The proper nourishment matters."

With the transformation of a caterpillar into a butterfly comes a change in how food is ingested and the type of nourishment required. The caterpillar's mouth is made to bite and chew, while the butterfly has a long coiled tube called a proboscis, used for siphoning nectars and water. Each type of butterfly is partial to the type of nectar it prefers, and it flies to its preferred environment in search of the proper nourishment necessary for the butterfly to thrive.

Like the discerning butterfly, as we emotionally and spiritually mature and transform, the type of nourishment that we need changes. Just as the butterfly flies in search of its preferred food source, we must spread our wings and travel in search of the appropriate nourishment—the things that nurture us and allow us to flourish.

Our nourishment might literally be the food we choose to eat, as our nutritional health does play a significant role in our emotional state. The less tangible things, however, that provide the proper nourishment might be the place we live, the vocation that we work at, or the people we surround ourselves with. The proper nourishment might be perceiving ourselves and the world optimistically, or giving ourselves and those around us the appropriate emotional rest and rejuvenation. All of these things play a distinct and important role in determining our overall emotional, spiritual, and physical health. All three are equally important so we may develop into the beautiful and individually unique person that we are meant to be. Making the effort to find what nurtures us is a worthwhile adventure—an adventure that is ongoing throughout life.

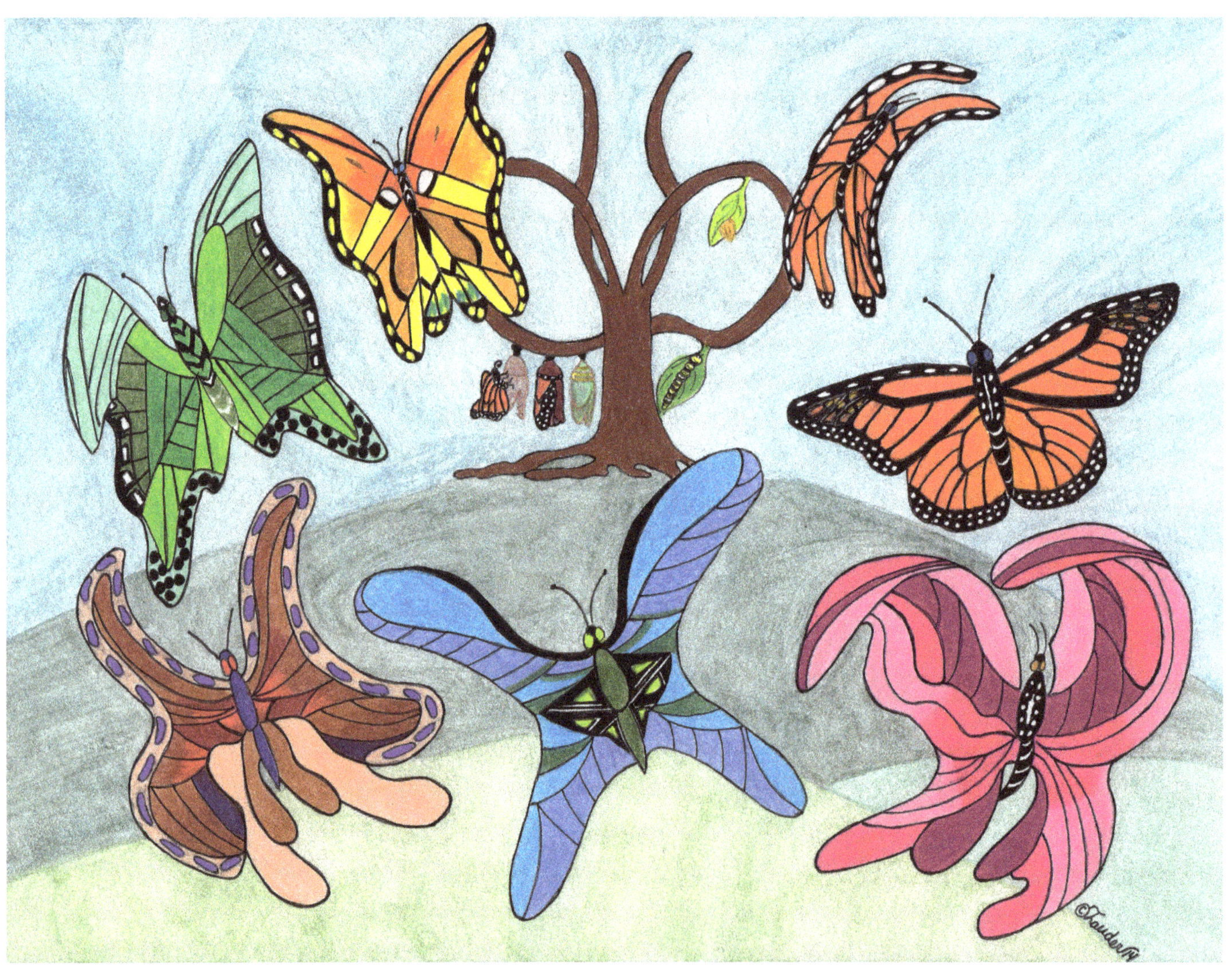

Butterfly: It's All in the Colors
"See me for who I really am."

Each type of butterfly has its own array of colors that makes it distinct, recognizable, beautiful, and provides it the protection it needs. The butterfly leaves its previous convoluted habitat behind and flies independently into any environment that embraces its arrival. Although some butterflies do have similar food preferences and behavioral patterns, each butterfly is very individual in all that fosters its optimal survival and preserves its uniqueness. Each takes a liberating flight in constant and necessary search of the various conditions and provisions which provide it life.

The act of the butterfly leaving its old habitat behind to fly to new places can be likened to the ongoing journey of human emotional and spiritual maturity. While it is frightening to let go and move beyond what feels familiar and safe, in order for our distinct features to be appreciated, we need to leave behind certain patterns, behaviors, or learned habits that prevent us from becoming the person we are meant to become. All that has been taught to us plays an essential role in our development and is necessary to teach us what we like and don't like, what feeds our soul and what destroys it, what we want to aspire to and what we never want to be like. We use what we have learned to become an individual. While our past is essential to our growth and development, it is something to learn from and not to dwell upon. The past allows us to become fully aware of what lies in front of us and to move purposefully and joyfully into the future. The present moment is all that we have with certainty.

Moving on from the familiar places where we feel bound may literally mean a physical change of location, as for the butterfly. It may, however, not mean a physical move at all. It may refer to a necessary change within our heads and our hearts. We might need to change our perceptions of things, our openness to others and to opportunities that we have not considered. Perhaps it means reviving old dreams and looking seriously and objectively at how they might be feasible. Moving on from something old may require us to accept ourselves for who we are and to embrace and foster that person, instead of always trying to be somebody we are not, whether for ourselves or for someone else. It might mean loving more and hating less, having more compassion and less frustration, more forgiveness and less anger. There are many ways to move away from the old and into the new. All lead to a journey of flight that is always changing, forever learning, and forever liberating.

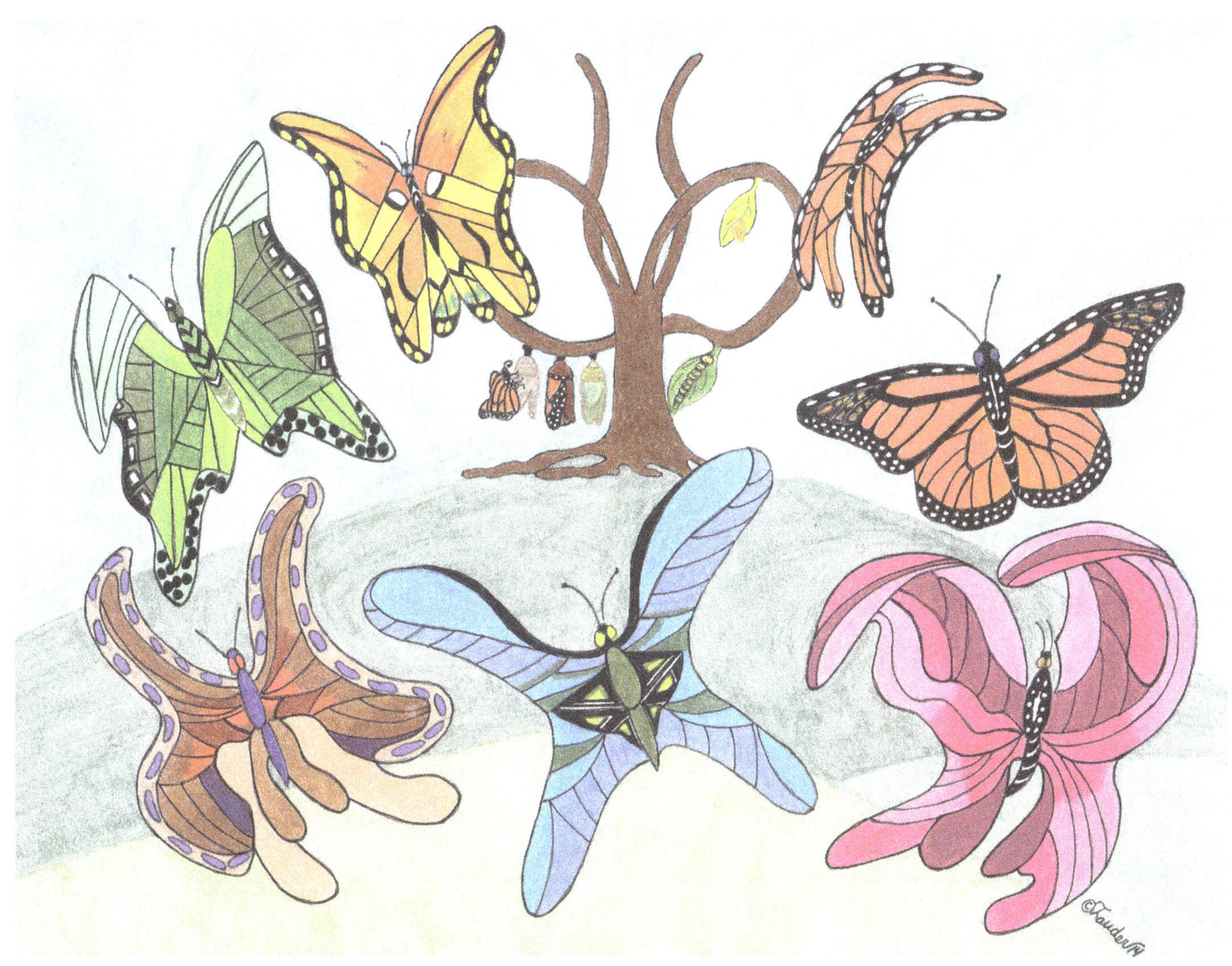

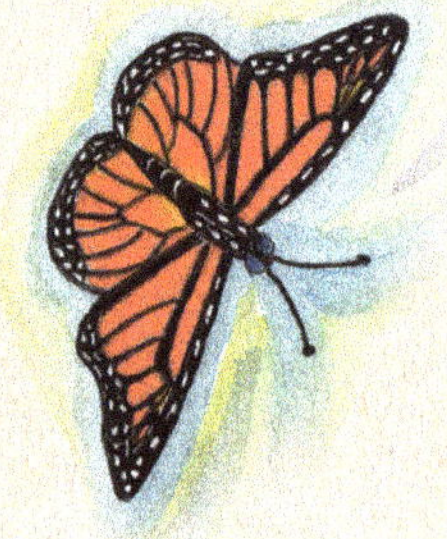
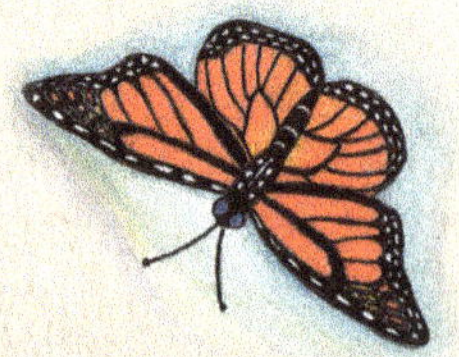

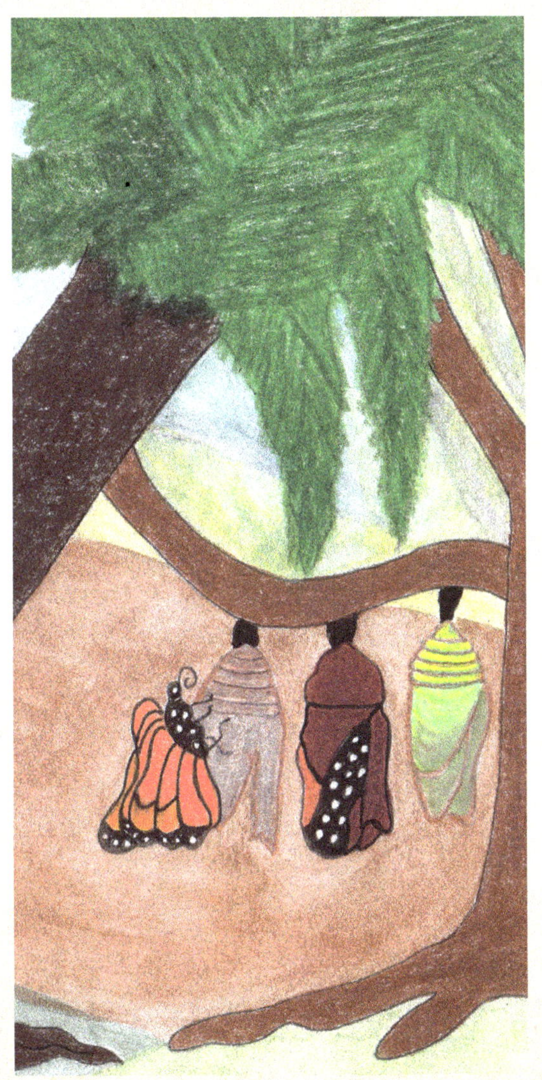

Section Two
Life is Challenging

The symbolic, convoluted tree pictured in the illustrations represents the place where all of the butterfly's stages of development take place.
The only way for the butterfly to leave its home is for it to progress through the convolutions within the tree, find an opening that leads away from what is familiar, and recognize that opening as an opportunity to fly through. As each butterfly leaves, it is unsure of what to expect. All of the butterfly's internal and external signals have given it confidence that it is prepared to enter a new environment. Life is full of challenges, however, for the butterfly and for ourselves. Things often get in the way of growth and development.

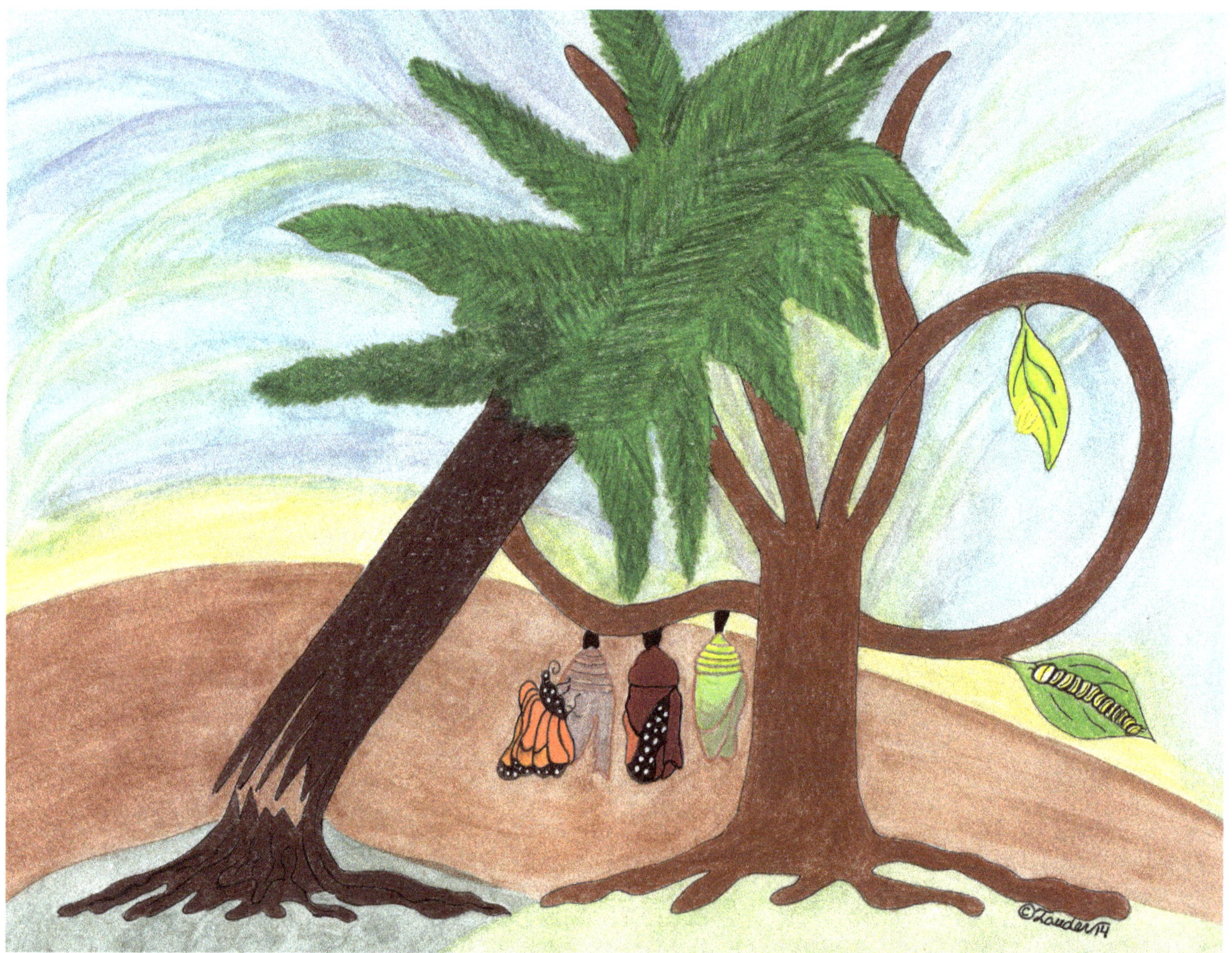

SUDDEN OBSTRUCTION
"Life's challenges can be harsh."

Some obstacles in life are sharp and harsh, and fall in the way suddenly, like the tree that has fallen over the butterfly's exit. They disrupt our path in life so completely that the option to continue in the same direction does not seem to exist. Such obstacles are obvious obstructions and easy to recognize. When this happens, it is easy to get discouraged and perhaps even give up on the notion of moving forward.

Sometimes these abrupt obstructions in our path are blessings in disguise and give us the unexpected but necessary time to reassess our choices and our directions in life. As humans, we have the intellect to consider that, with assistance, we may be able to clear the obstruction and continue on the path we originally intended to take. Our other option, however, is to find a new and perhaps less troublesome and more fulfilling route to travel.

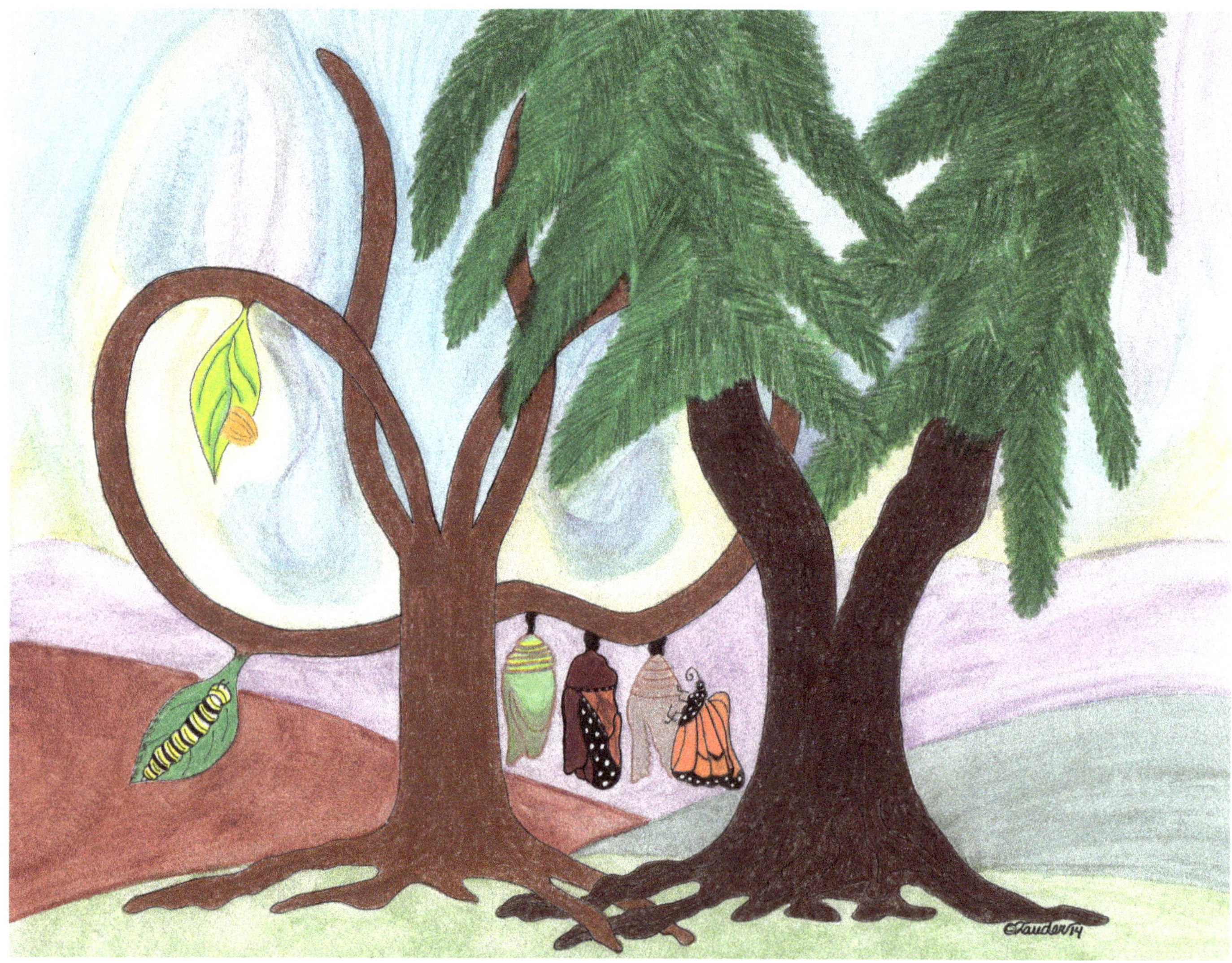

OPTICAL ILLUSION
"Life's challenges can be confusing and deceiving."

Other times, challenges in life that alter continued growth, development, and final flight are less obvious. Things are a bit confusing. The two-headed tree has grown beside the butterfly's habitat for years. It looks like all of the other trees of its kind from where the butterfly has resided for three cycles of its life. Only when the butterfly is ready for flight does it realize that its area of exit is not wide open or obvious. It appears to be blocked. The newly emerged butterfly will still be able to fly out through its normal exit, but it will take the butterfly more time to realize that there is still room to move through and fly.

Similarly, we may be ready to move forward with or away from something in life—ready to fly. We consider our situation, and our initial assessment tells us that our path is blocked. We don't immediately recognize that our passageway is only partially obstructed, because we are tired from the energy required to build up enough strength to have the courage to leave the place where we feel stuck. Often it is our own fears or self-doubt that makes us blind to the reality of the situation. After a time of rest and reassessment, however, we notice the small but feasible opening. Movement away from what looks normal, but instinctively does not feel right, is possible. The opportunity for exit is still present, but the passageway is narrower and will require a little innovation and perhaps some help.

As long as the butterfly stays within its familiar environment, it will never experience anything different in life and never realize that other evergreen trees grow straight and normally don't block the exit like this two-headed tree does. While the two-headed tree's appearance looks like all of the other trees in the distance, it is really a deceiving variation of normal that makes the butterfly feel trapped. Once the butterfly leaves its familiar habitat and flies within its new environment, it can recognize the reality of its situation. The same holds true for us. Only when we leave our previous environment and view things from a different vantage point are we able to differentiate the normal-appearing situation for the variation of normal that it really is.

For us, the two-headed tree might represent something as straight-forward as being in the wrong place in life for who we are and where our passions and talents lie. Perhaps it is a job that does not fit our personality, or that we hate but was expected of us. The two-headed tree might be an abusive or controlling household situation that nobody else is aware of. You might live with a handicap in which you have been led to believe by yourself or others that many options in life are not possible. Variations of normal can be confusing and deceiving and often require help.

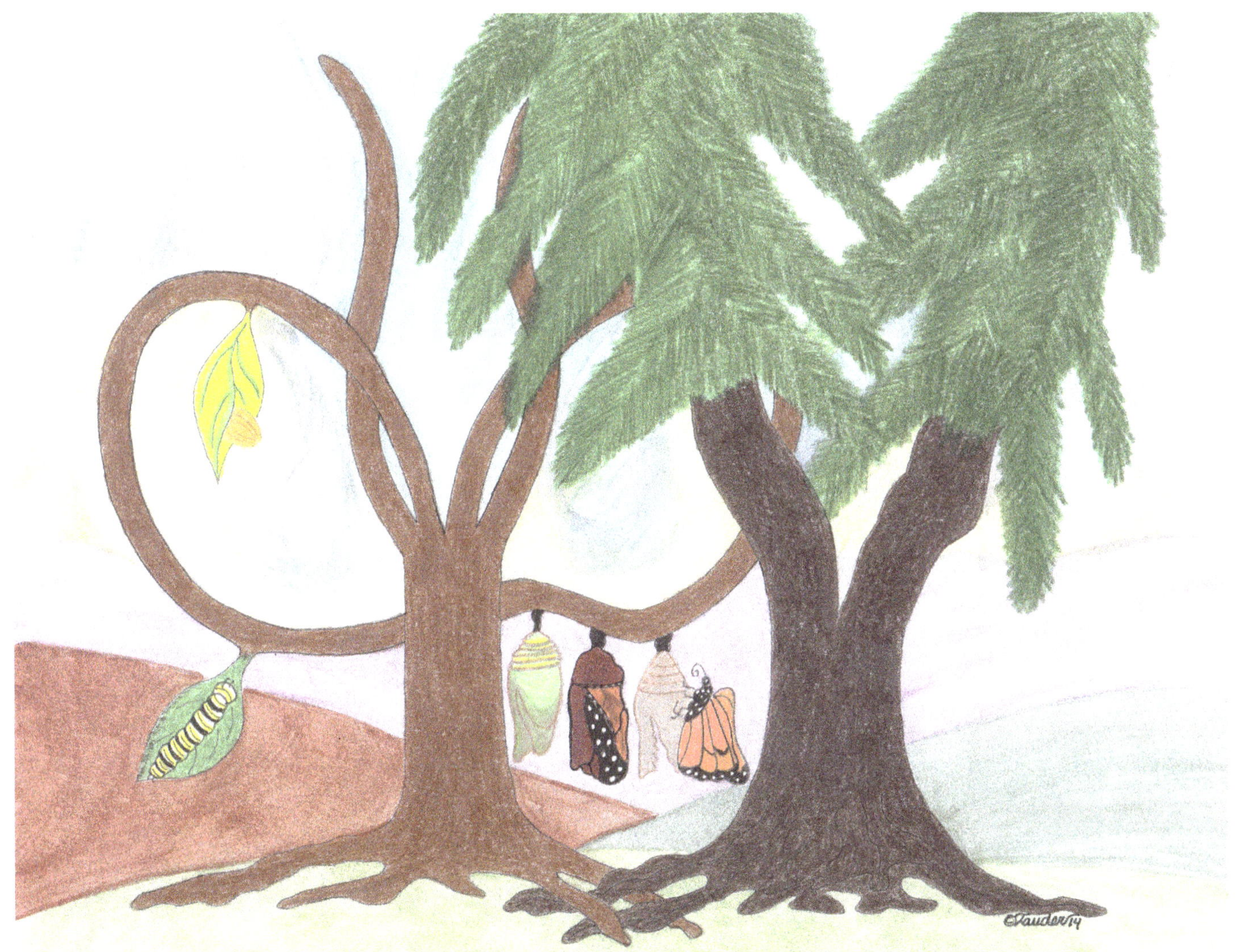

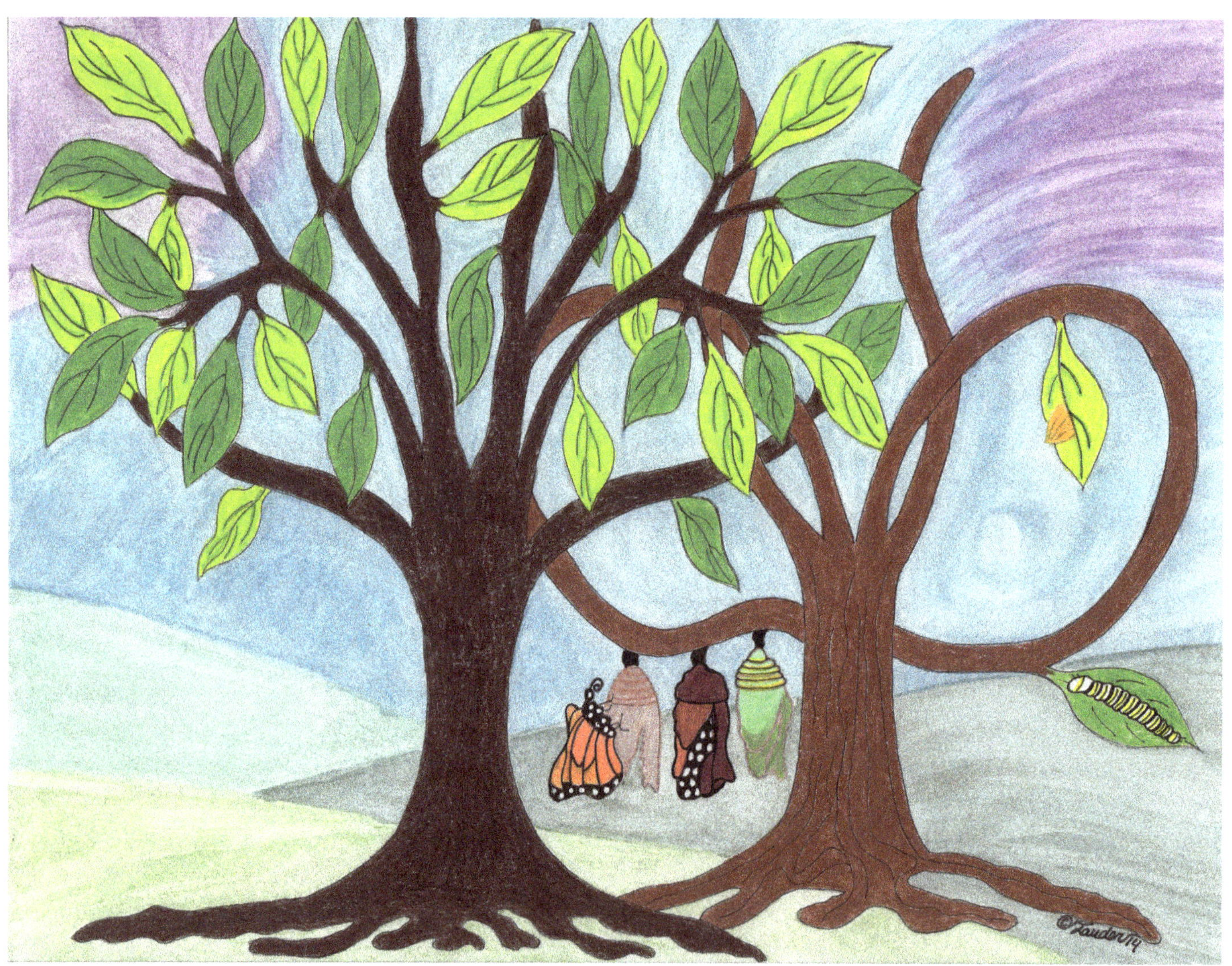

OVERBEARING BRANCHES
"Life's challenges can be something normal and in our midst all along."

Other things in life are such slow, progressive hindrances that they can block growth and development without our awareness. The majestic leafy tree that has so naturally grown beside the butterfly tree for years has slowly enlarged, spread out, and overtaken the butterfly's opportunity for exit, flight, and continued development. Until some of the leaves can be cleared, the butterfly has no way out. It will continue to cling to the chrysalis—the familiar place where it feels safe.

For us, a number of different obstacles are similar to the leafy tree. They are things in life that are a normal part of our environment, familiar to what we know, and have been exposed to. They grow so slowly over time that we do not recognize them as obstructions. As time goes on, these things crowd and invade our developmental path. Not knowing any differently, we perceive that our only option is to stay where we are.

A slow-growing hindrance might be well-meaning people who view the world from their experiences. They can only imagine that their opinions are the only way to think or do things. Sometimes harboring old hurts and offenses can hold us in the past so tightly that we cannot see the life right in front of us, much less imagine a future that looks any different from what we have already experienced. Another slow-growing hindrance might be our perceptions of things—ourselves, the people around us, and the world. While real and true in our own mind, our perceptions of things may not always be accurate or based on fact. Whether one of the above examples or your own personal situation, all are things that can interfere with our forward emotional and spiritual progression in life.

Before we can overcome such obstacles, we must first recognize that an obstacle exists. Recognizing and overcoming inconspicuous barriers in life usually requires help, and help can present itself in many different ways.

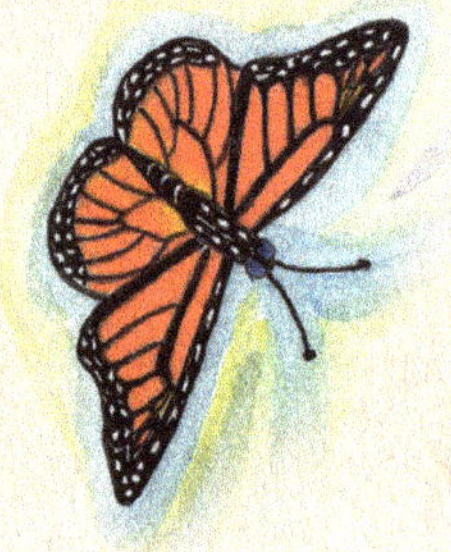

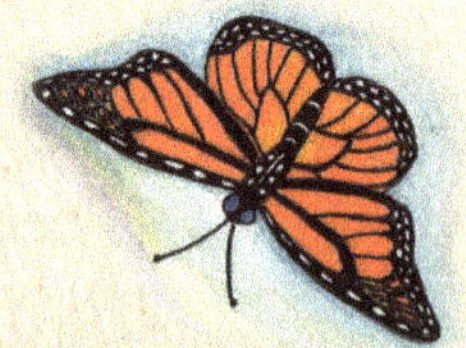

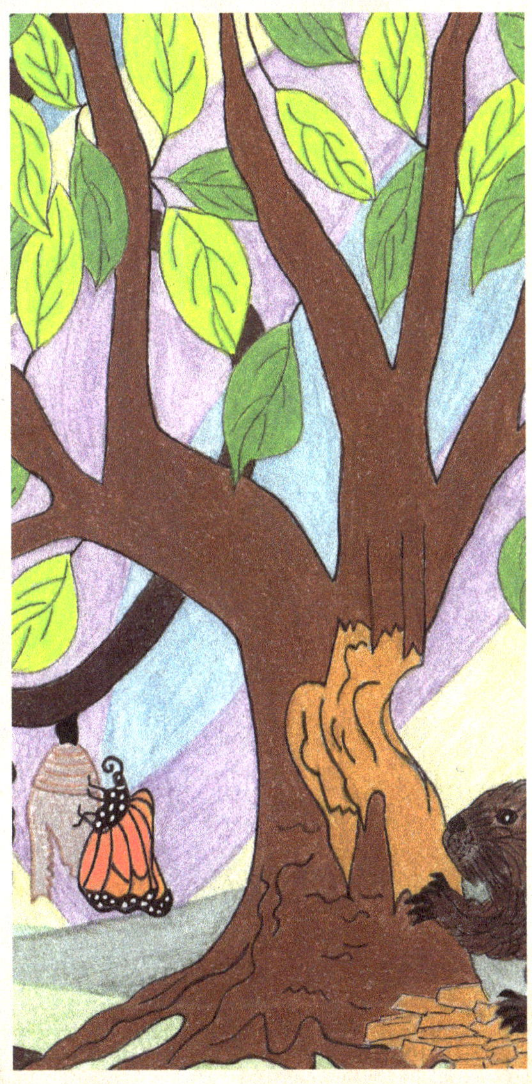

<h1>3
SECTION THREE
Help is Everywhere If You Look</h1>

Regardless of the type of challenges that come our way, a helping hand is always a welcome gift, and many times is essential for our growth. For some obstacles in life, the need for help is obvious and easy to accept. Recognizing the less obvious obstacles in our development, however, can be challenging and may also require help from others.

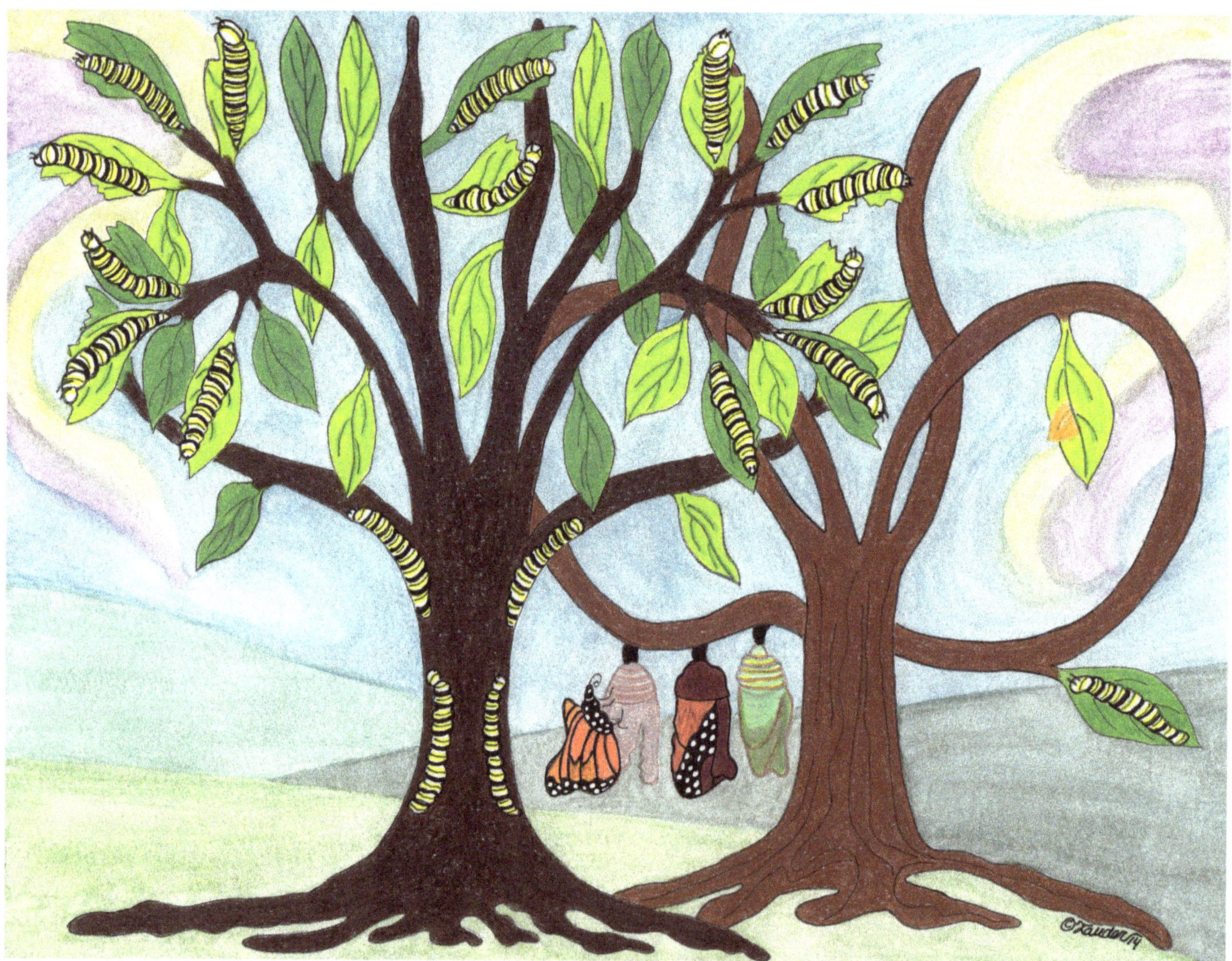

Friendly Faces
"Help can be something familiar."

Help often comes from those we know and recognize. They can see what will hamper or has hampered our forward progression in life and can help clear our path. The caterpillars in this picture are creatures familiar to the butterfly. In the caterpillars' active state of eating, they can easily and happily help clear the obstacles from the butterfly's path of flight. The butterfly clinging to the chrysalis may not even be aware that a problem exists, and may even view the caterpillar's presence as a threat to its familiar habitat. It is not until the butterfly's counterparts slowly eat away the obstacle that the complacent butterfly begins to see the opening being created.

Similar to the butterfly's situation, often those who know us or perhaps are only acquaintances can see that our path in life is blocked, even though we don't recognize it ourselves. These familiar people see us and our situation from a different vantage point, and can offer us various insights about ourselves and our situation. They can objectively assess our reaction to different things and situations, getting a better sense of what makes us thrive and what puts us in a bad place emotionally. They can see our passions and sense our dislikes. They can see when we try too hard and perhaps, not hard enough. They can tell when we have become complacent, instead of aspiring to expand ourselves. They can give us a perspective on what we have already accomplished in life and remind us that we are capable of continuing forward.

Lots of advice and opinions will come our way in one lifetime from those we know. The intentions behind all of the information may not always be straightforward or correct. The important part is to be willing to hear what others have to say, take the time to reflect upon their advice, and put it into context with who we are and the situation that we are in. Not all help offered to us may be done for the right reasons, but it might still offer an unexpected blessing. For example, the caterpillars in this picture may just be eating the leaves away because they are hungry, instead of the fact that they see the leaves as a hindrance to the butterfly's flight path. The fact that they eat the leaves away, however, still provides the butterfly with a positive outcome—a clear path for flight. Anything in life can be our guide if we take the time to assess what comes our way and put it into its proper perspective.

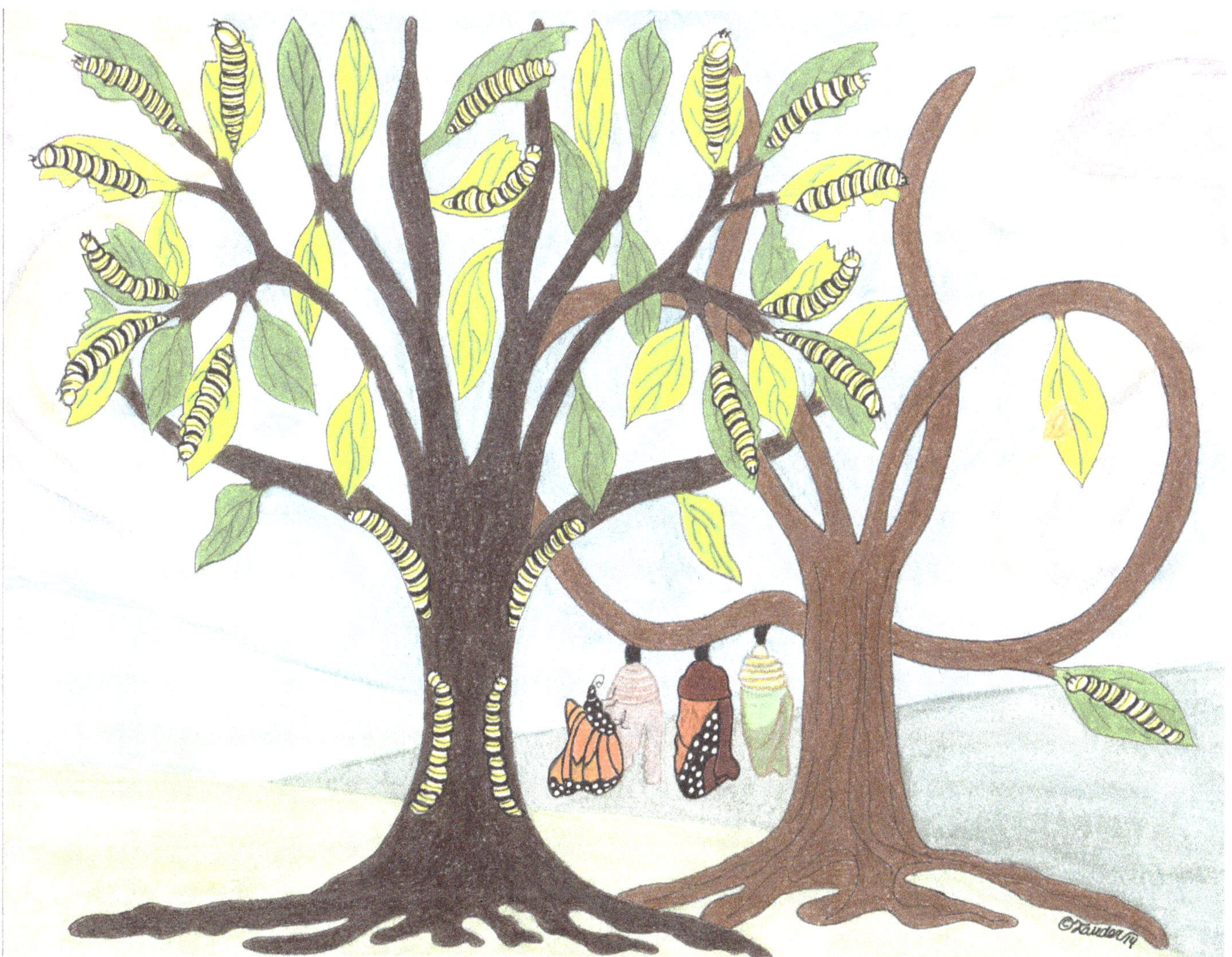

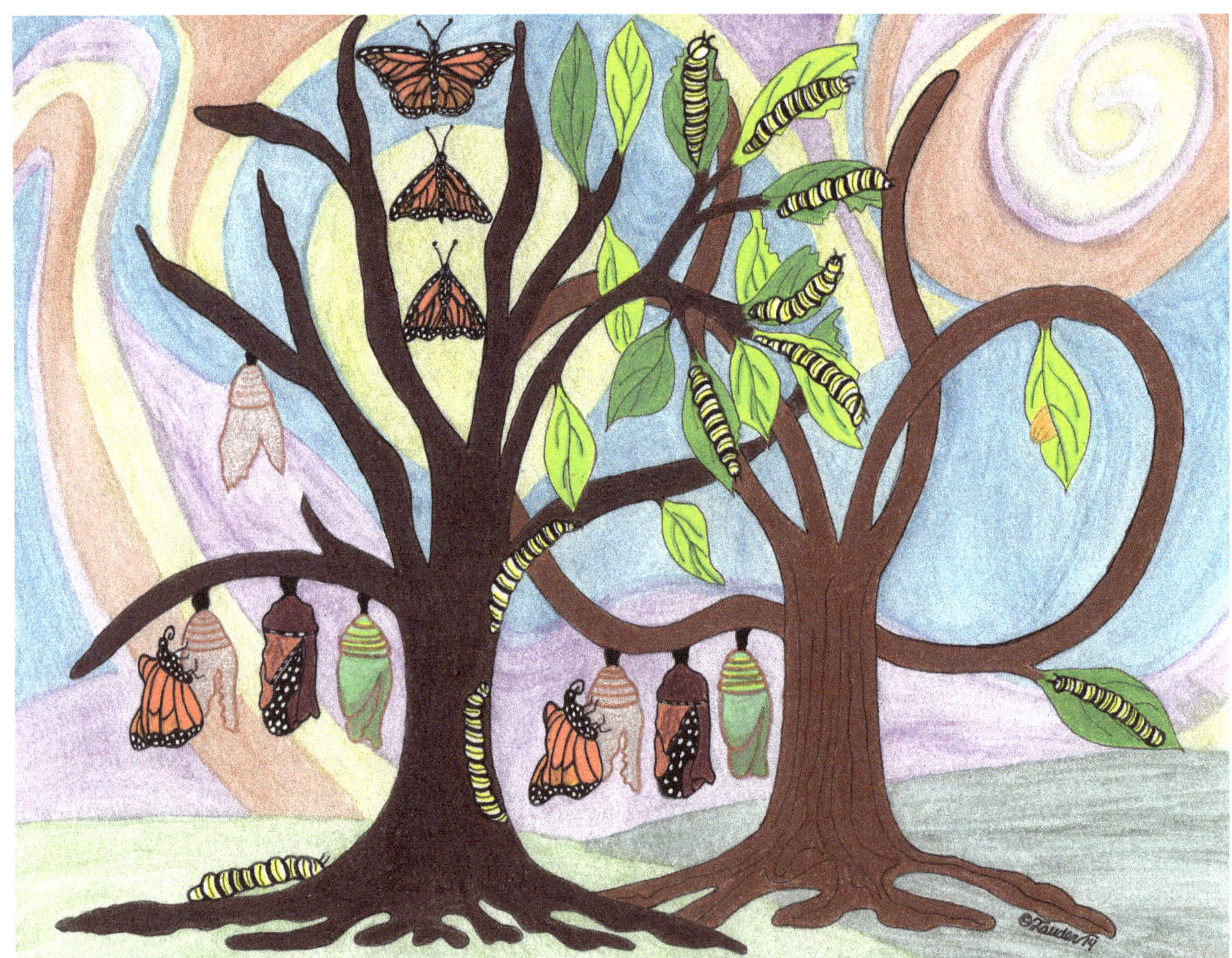

CONSIDERABLE OPTIONS
"Help can be taking an alternative route."

Sometimes, rather than helping to clear the expected path for us, others can show us how to maneuver through alternative and narrow passageways in order to continue forward. They have found other paths that have allowed them to open their wings and fly. They share their experiences so that we can learn a new way of dealing with a challenge.

The butterflies on the left have found a different route from which to fly. In fact, they have taken residence in a different habitat completely. Their place of flight is not as wide and does not look the same as what the butterfly on the right was expecting, but their alternative route allows them to move into the big world with their flight wings open wide.

There are always people who come our way with experiences different from our own. The gift they offer is a different set of skills and knowledge. They can teach us how to take acceptable, alternative routes in life—routes that we never thought of or experienced before. The key is to allow ourselves to be open to new ways of approaching and thinking about things. Instead of dismissing their ideas as wrong, we need to appreciate what others offer as being different than our own experience. From others, we can learn the process of growth, forward progression, and flight, by watching and respecting their examples.

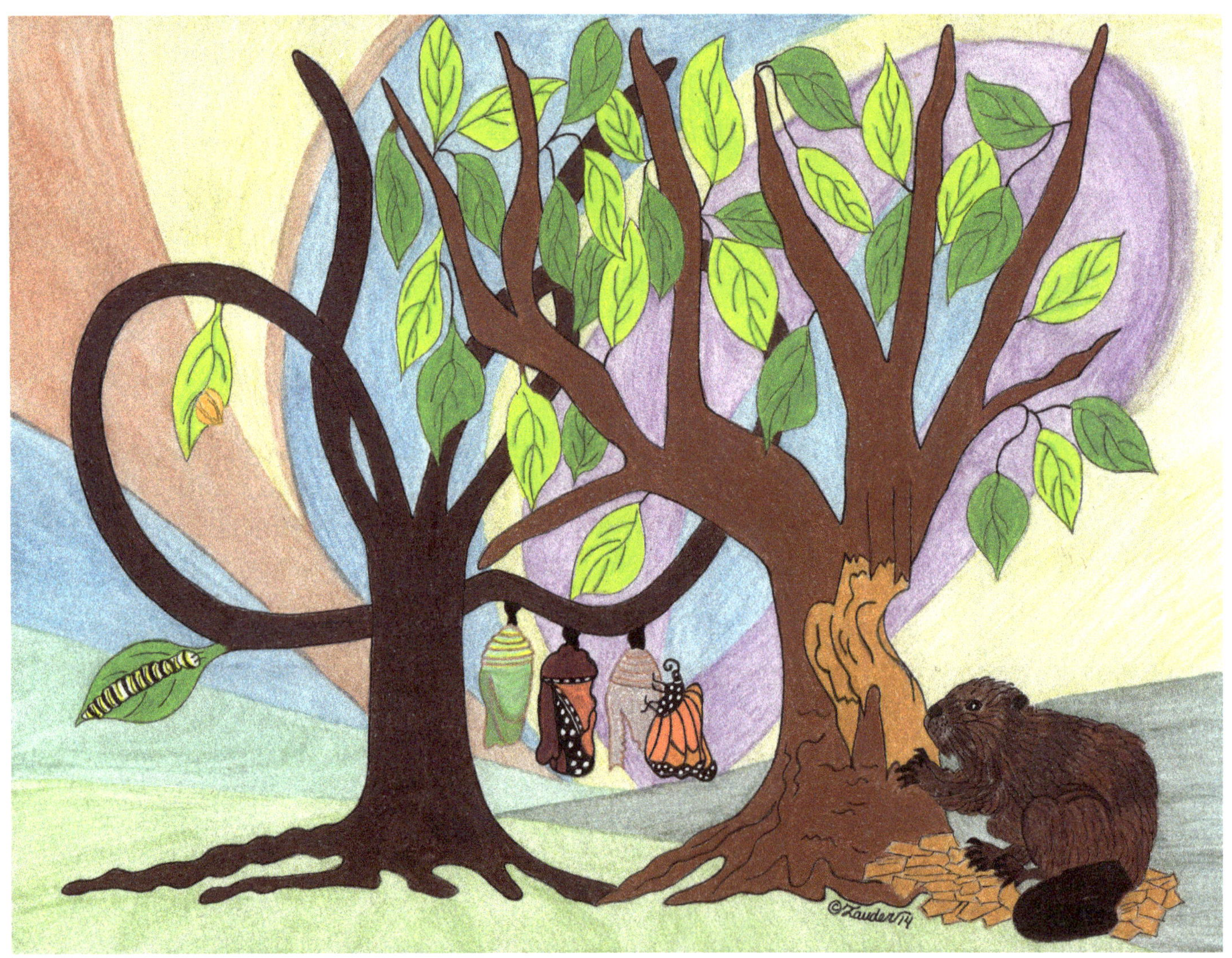

STRANGER THINGS HAPPEN
"Help can be the unfamiliar."

Other times, the help that is needed comes from those we do not know or recognize. The beaver is unfamiliar to the butterfly which has just emerged from the chrysalis. The butterfly is unaware of what a beaver is or what it is capable of. The butterfly's initial instinct is to be fearful of this unfamiliar creature and to fly away. The exit path is blocked, however, by the leaves of the tree, so the butterfly's reaction is to cling tighter to its familiar torn chrysalis. As time passes, the loud noise and flying wooden debris that the beaver creates make the butterfly see the beaver as only an annoying presence rather than a potential threat.

If we are like the butterfly, our initial reaction to the unfamiliar is one of rejection. We are afraid of the unfamiliar and we may cling even more tightly to what we know. A turning point in our growth, however, is when we learn to assess before we react. Unlike our childhood curiosity and fearlessness, as adults we tend to enter into situations with preconceived notions, and sometimes skepticism, allowing ourselves to become stuck in the same old place. Similar to the butterfly's change of opinion about the beaver, with the passage of time we too may see the unfamiliar differently.

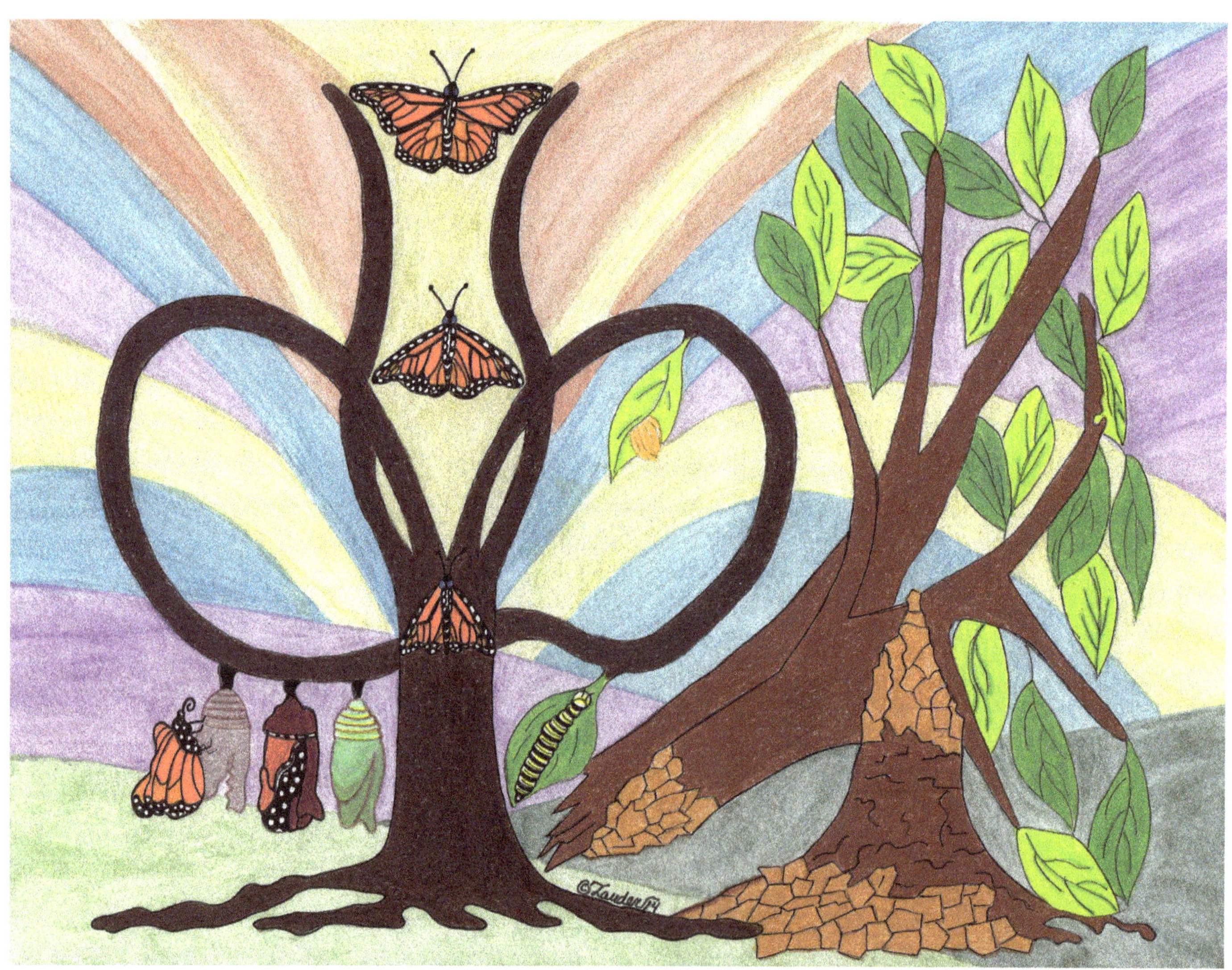

STRANGER REVELATIONS
"The unfamiliar can help in unexpected ways."

Little did the butterfly know that the unfamiliar creature in its midst would be able to clear a path for it to fly. Because the beaver causes an abrupt clearing, the butterfly immediately can see the sunshine through the obvious opening and knows exactly where to go.

Sometimes life is like that. Help comes from something or someone that we don't expect and clarifies our next step in life. It might be people that we do not know. Perhaps it is just a simple statement of inspiration or encouragement from a book, a television show, or movie. Clarity may come to us by seeing a beautiful sight in nature. In order to recognize these unexpected gifts, however, we must keep an open mind that anything in the world can act to assist us. The smallest and perhaps the most unexpected and inconspicuous thing, statement, or person can help us clear our blocks, hindrances, or fears that have halted our forward progression in life. When we live life with our eyes, our ears, and our hearts wide open, anything can help us mature into the people that we aspire to become.

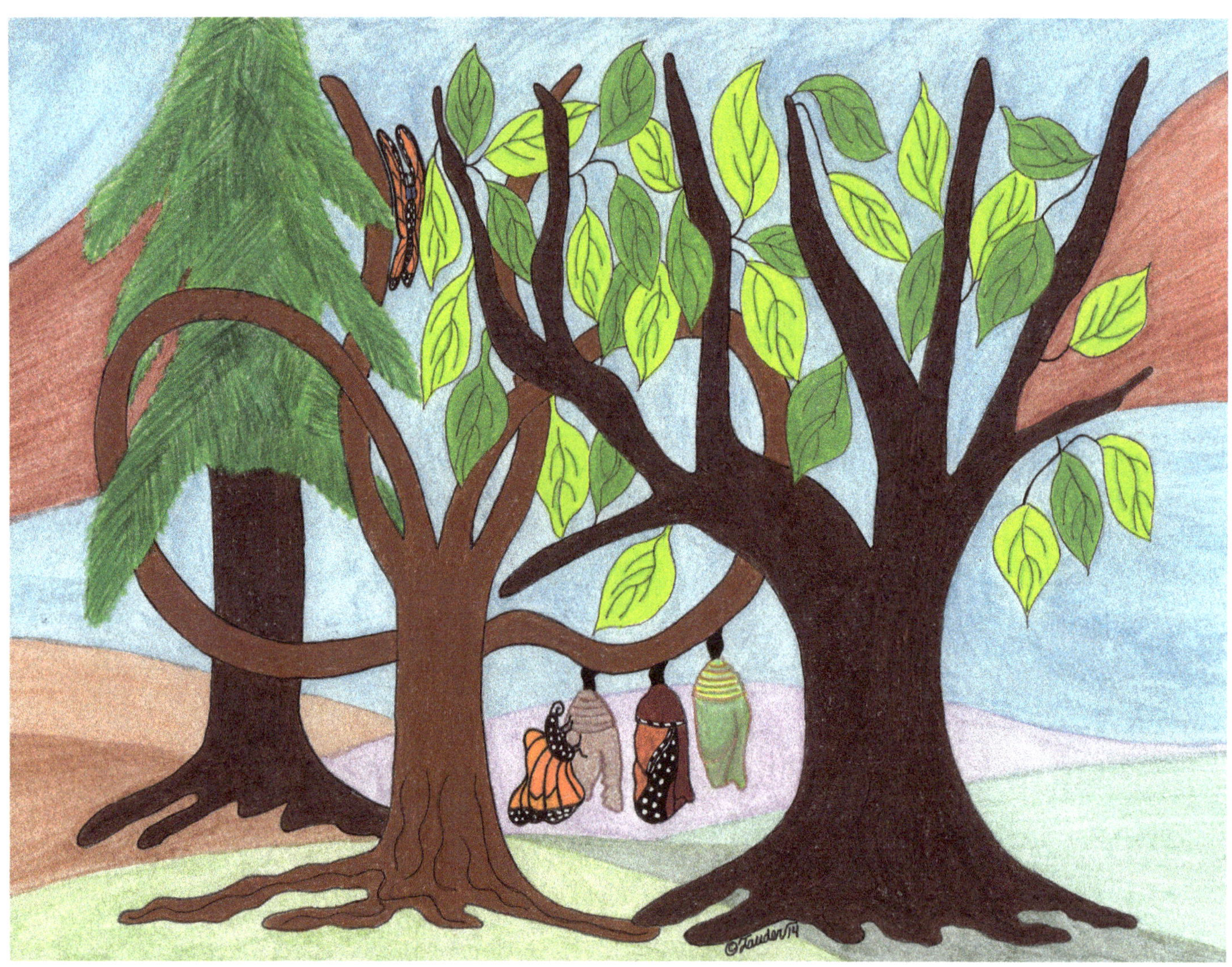

Working it Out
"Sometimes we figure things out for ourselves."

Despite difficult challenges in life, we can learn to overcome the odds against us and find the strength to break free from the things that block our path. At times, we instinctively feel strong enough to continue our emotional and spiritual journey. Everything within us and outside of us feels right. It seems as if a Higher Power is telling us that we are ready to move on—that we are ready for new growth. Even though our path appears blocked and it feels as if help is not available, or perhaps it came and went without our knowledge, we feel prepared.

At first glance, the butterfly in this picture sees no available exit. After some time of contemplation, the butterfly begins to recognize where its normal place of exit is supposed to be. The exit appears blocked by the leafy tree, and no recognizable or unexpected help has come along. The butterfly has the option to wait for help, but instead, it chooses to change its form temporarily until it is almost unrecognizable, in order to squeeze out of its comfortable, but confined, environment. Instinctively, it knows that the timing is right. It is aware that the only place that it can open its wings fully to fly is into the vast blue sky above.

Similarly for us, at times in our life it is up to us to navigate away from our zone of comfort and safety. It is the only way that we can venture to a place that allows room for us to be our true selves. Our travel through the tight exit might require us to "change our shape." We might have to temporarily do things out of the ordinary for us by taking a calculated risk, making ourselves and perhaps our hearts a bit vulnerable, or conforming to our current environment in order to safely leave it behind. Life confronts all of us with certain obligations and requirements, but these do not require us to stop pursuing our higher purpose in life—the higher plan for which we were created.

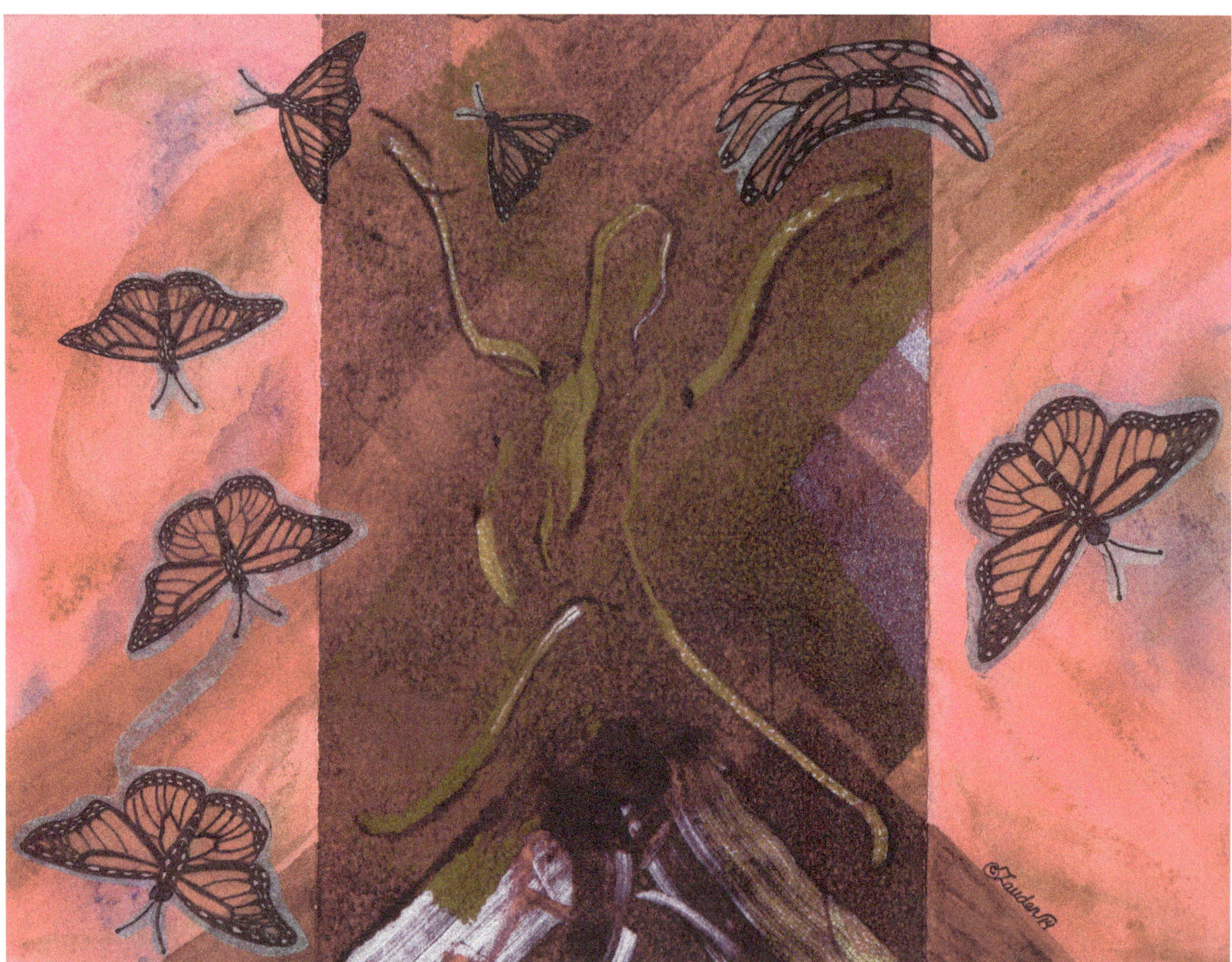

BREAKING FREE TOO
"If the butterfly can do it, so can you."

The butterfly flies throughout its life and begins its life cycle all over again by leaving a piece of itself behind to bring new life. The butterfly leaves an egg before it dies. As humans, whether we leave behind children, or a piece of ourselves by touching someone else's life, we can only do it by flying free—being true to the person that we were created to be. With death comes life. With the death of the butterfly comes another butterfly and the cycle begins all over again. With the release of each fear and old restraint that binds us in a negative place, comes the birth of a new part of ourselves, and the cycle begins all over again.

The next time you see a butterfly, notice the freedom and grace with which it floats through the air. We can't train a butterfly, but we can train ourselves to become more like one. It takes great fortitude to break free from the forces that bind us.

"Most of us never consider how powerful the creator really is. Instead, we draw very limited amounts of the power available to us. We decide how powerful God is for us. We unconsciously set a limit on how much God can give us or help us." Julia Cameron[3]

"Ask and it will be given you; seek and you will find; knock and it will be opened to you." Matthew 7:7 RSV[4]

"Comfort will often keep us from growth." John Ortberg[5]

"We understand that leaving the comforts of where we are and what we know is not easy. Transformation is never easy—and transformation is what the journey promises." Joseph Dispenza[6]

"Feeling and releasing our fears on a regular basis—sometimes before taking each step—is how we move forward and into the next dimension in our lives." Melody Beattie[7]

"The punishment imposed on us for claiming true self can never be worse than the punishment we impose on ourselves by failing to make that claim." Parker Palmer[8]

"The first step toward personal freedom is awareness. We need to be aware that we are not free in order to be free." Don Miguel Ruiz[9]

"The challenging thing about flying—like living—is that you never learn everything." Katharine Jefferts Schori[10]

"Everybody is a genius. But if you judge a fish by its ability to climb a tree, it will live its whole life believing that it is stupid." Albert Einstein[11]

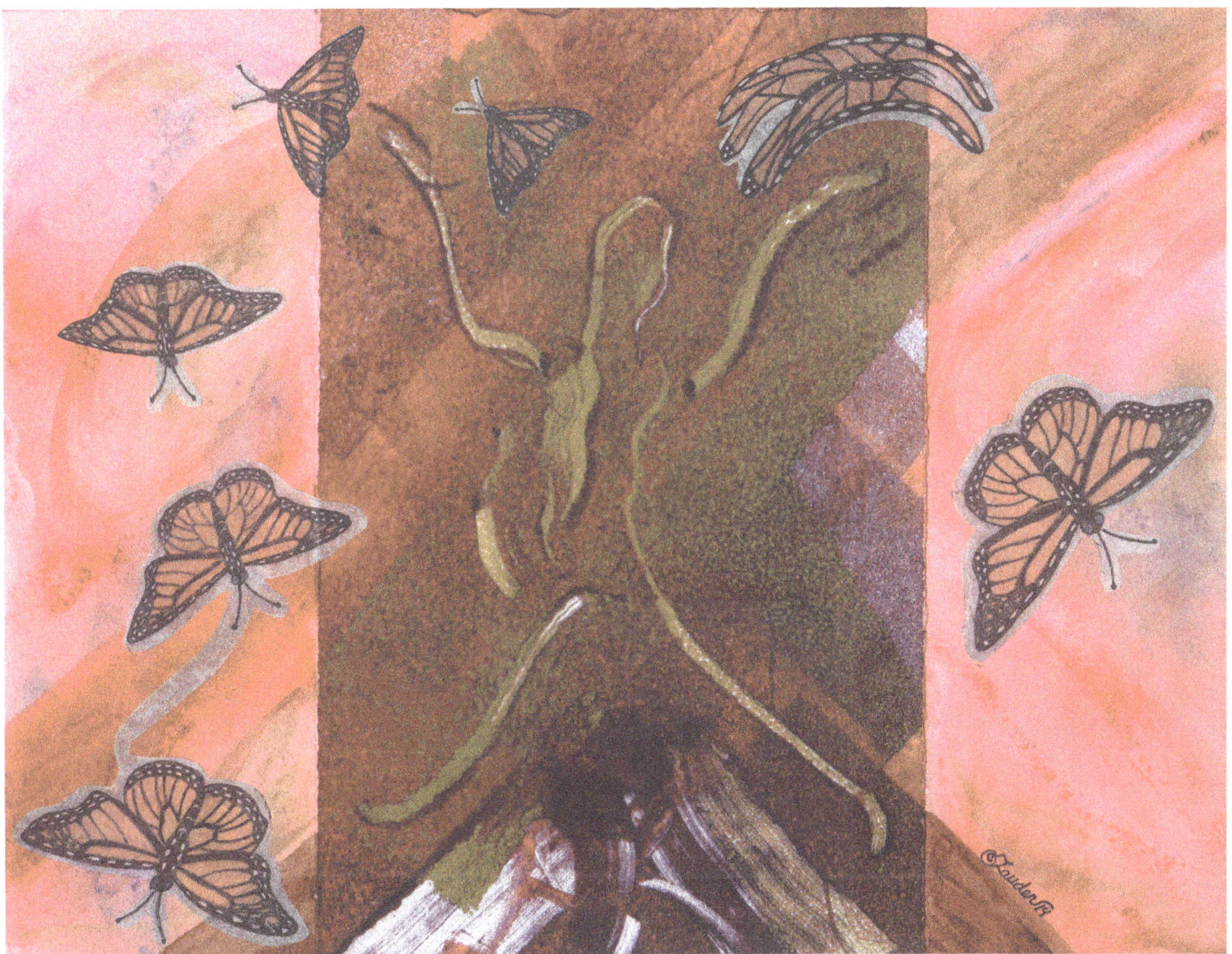

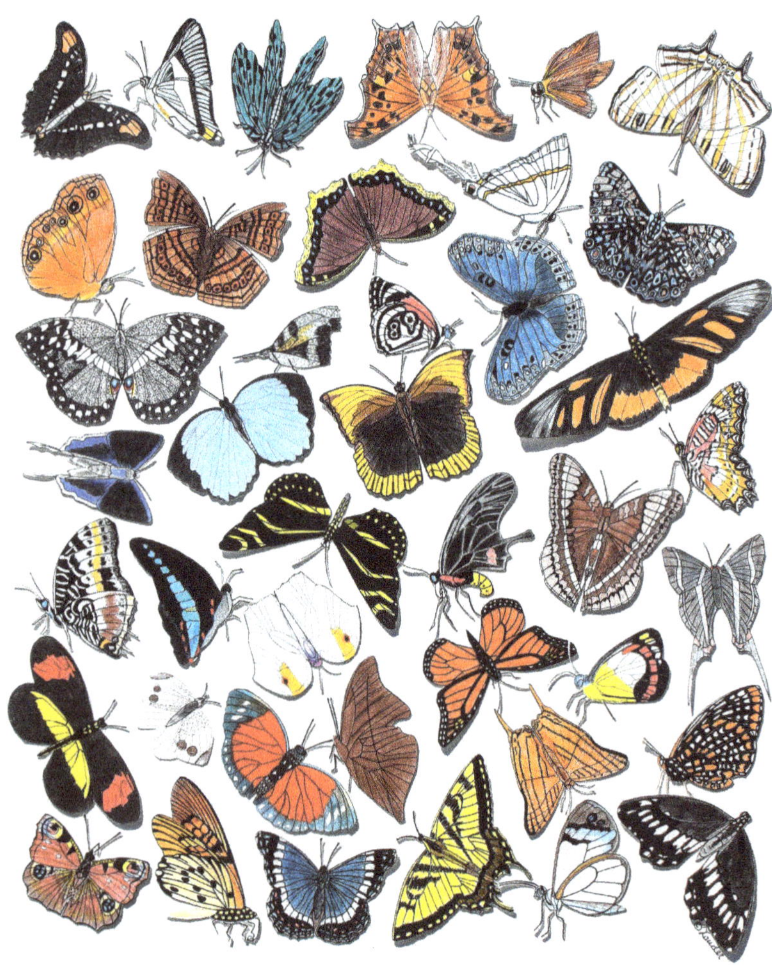

YOU ARE BEAUTIFUL [12-14]
"You are beautiful too."

You were created talented and individually recognizable. Take the time for silence and self-reflection. Foster your growth and development so that you too can fly with freedom and grace throughout the world like the butterfly. You are uniquely beautiful.

"You Are Beautiful"
by
Tamara Lauder

References and Credits

1. J. Burris and W. Richards, *The Life Cycles of Butterflies*; North Adams, MA: Storey Publishing, 2006.

2. C. Kiefers, © iStock Photo file #2778741, Calgary, Alberta, Canada.

3. J. Cameron, *The Artist's Way: A Spiritual Path to Higher Creativity*; New York, NY: Jeremy P. Tarcher/Putnam a member of Penguin Putnam Inc., 1992, p.91.

4. *The Holy Bible: Revised Standard Version*; Grand Rapids, MI: Zondervan Publishing House, 1946, Matthew 7:7, p.12 of New Testament section.

5. J. Ortberg, *If You Want To Walk On Water, You've Got To Get Out Of The Boat*; Grand Rapids, MI: Zondervan, 2001, p. 46.

6. J. Dispenza, *The Way Of The Traveler: Making Every Trip a Journey of Self-Discovery*; Emeryville, CA: Avalon Travel Publishing, 1999, p. 22.

7. M. Beattie, *Finding Your Way Home: A Soul Survival Kit*; New York, NY: HarperSanFrancisco, a division of HarperCollins Publishers, 1998, p. 169.

8. P. J. Palmer, *Let Your Life Speak: Listening for the Voice of Vocation*; San Francisco, CA: Jossey-Bass Inc. Publishers, 2000, p.34.

9. D. Miguel Ruiz, *The Four Agreements*; San Rafael, CA: Amber-Allen Publishing, 1997, p.98.

10. K. Jefferts Schori, *A Wing and a Prayer: A Message of Faith and Hope*; Harrisburg, NY: Morehouse Publishing, 2007, p.101.

11. A. Einstein, *25 Phenomenal Albert Einstein Quotes*; posted by Ali Rehman on September, 28th 2013 http://graphicsheat.com/albert-einstein-quotes/

12. L. Weber, *Butterflies of the North Woods*; Duluth, MN: Kollath + Stensaas Publishing, Ed.2, 2006.

13. J. Glassberg, *Butterflies of North America*; New York, NY: Sterling Publishing, 2011.

14. K. Preston-Mafham, *500 Butterflies From Around the World*; Buffalo, NY: C Brown Reference Group 2007, © now held by Brown Bear Books.

About the Author

All of her life Tamara felt compelled to capture the world's splendor and symbolism through creativity. Raised in the rural community of South Dakota, she was immersed in the beauty, mystery, and unpredictability of nature. Although her life's work as a physician took her from coast to coast and blessed her with a diversity of experiences, her unyielding passion for art called her to places she had not yet traveled. After seventeen years of an academic medicine career in the specialty of Physical Medicine and Rehabilitation, Tamara left the practice of medicine from the walls of an institution, to follow her own dream of becoming a full-time professional artist and providing healing through the arts.

Today, she lives in the Northwoods of Wisconsin and works as a professional artist. She spends the majority of her time in pottery and printmaking, but also creates artforms using other mediums. Tamara has published numerous medical publications, and enjoys including inspirational and informational writings for the pottery and two-dimensional pieces that she creates. Her love of the outdoors and her favorite activities of biking, running, cross-country skiing, and snowshoeing are the creative catalysts for her work.